For ten years, Buck Rodgers was vice-president of marketing, with responsibility for IBM's worldwide marketing activities. In 1984 he took early retirement, but he still serves the corporation as a consultant. Renowned within company circles as a motivator, articulator of ideas and practitioner of excellence, Rodgers is equally well known as a public speaker. 'When you listen to Buck Rodgers speak,' write the authors of *In Search of Excellence*, 'there's a feeling of déjà vu, and you suddenly realize you are listening to the modern incarnation of [IBM founder] Watson insisting on the Golden Rule [of service].'

At home, Buck Rodgers manages to find time for civic activities and sports (he is a low-handicap golfer, an avid tennis player and a dedicated runner). He and his wife, Helen, have three children, all of whom work for IBM.

The IBM Way

Insights into the World's Most Successful Marketing Organization

F. G. 'BUCK' RODGERS
with Robert L. Shook

FONTANA/Collins

First published by Harper & Row, Publishers, Inc. 1986
First published in Fontana Paperbacks 1989

THE IBM WAY Copyright © 1986 by Francis G. Rogers
and Robert L. Shook
Foreword Copyright © 1986 by Harper & Row, Publishers, Inc.

Printed and bound in Great Britain by
William Collins Sons & Co. Ltd, Glasgow

4/10/93

This book is dedicated to
Helen, Christy Ann, Scott and Kathy.
They have been my love, joy and inspiration.

CONTENTS

CONTENTS

FOREWORD

By Thomas J. Peters

'IBM has been built on some simple ideas and principles . . . like thoughtfulness, courtesy and integrity.'
Buck Rodgers, IBM's top marketing executive for ten
years, provides the first comprehensive behind-the-
scenes look at marketing in the world's most successful company. The secrets he reveals are obvious, as the
above passage suggests. Yet in my view they are the
clear-cut reasons, oddly hidden from competitors,
which explain IBM's tremendous success.

I hope that one chapter title rings in the ears of every
American manager: 'Creating a Totally Sales-Oriented
Environment'. Rodgers speaks with dismay of the
many companies that take their people and their
customers for granted. He talks about a different world
at IBM: 'The Company Heroes' are the marketing
people – IBM's VIPs. The logic: 'Let's face it, the
salesperson is the source from which everything in
business starts.' Moreover, *everyone* is involved in
sales at IBM. Every job description in the various
marketing divisions – even accounting and personnel
– spells out a 'customer connection' with the customer
orientation being part of every performance evaluation.
Engineers, financial people, and executives alike are
regularly in the field. And heaven help the IBM branch
managers who fail to keep in touch with their top
customers.

The sales orientation, though, is just the beginning.

The relationship with the customer is what ultimately counts: 'Most companies are a lot better at prospecting for new customers and selling those prospects than they are at maintaining the existing customer base.' With that, Rodgers lays out the Alpha to Omega of IBM's awesome approach to service.

These are the simple but impressive themes. The supporting details are there by the bucketful: job descriptions, account review processes, quota setting, recognition programs, the ins and outs of IBM's compensation plans, training, recruiting, customer listening. He goes so far as to describe such little touches as having the marketing reps introduce the local IBM accounts-receivable team to their customers. Everybody becomes a part of the IBM-customer bandwagon.

I have been accused regularly of having discovered the obvious; one very successful business person even went so far as to call my work a 'blinding flash of the obvious'. Buck Rodgers could be tarred with the same brush. And I presume he will be as delighted as I. From grocery chains to steel companies to car dealerships, when I have observed excellence it has always resulted from applying common sense and common courtesy – to one's people and one's customers. And this is Rodgers' message.

It's hard to complicate the message. One wonders, then, why so few follow – and, more important, persist at – these common sense strictures. I don't know, frankly. We seem to have become so ensnared in complexity that we have lost sight of these basics.

There is, it is clear, a revolution afoot. Companies and their managers are fundamentally rethinking their approaches to doing business. What they most need is a role model. There can be none better than IBM; there can be no better role model or voice than thirty-four-year veteran executive (1950–1984) Buck Rodgers. He saw and led through IBM's growth from $250 million to $50 billion. We can all consider ourselves lucky for his having laid bare the IBM marketing story. It's simple. I just hope we listen – and act on what Buck says.

ACKNOWLEDGMENTS

During the past few years, I began to think about the possibility of writing a book – not an autobiography, but a book about the IBM corporation and the subject of marketing. Every now and then, my family would urge me on, as would some close friends inside and outside IBM.

The more contact I had with customers, universities and industry associations, the more convinced I became that IBM's story was a special one and that others could benefit from what this corporation and its people do on a day-to-day basis. Also, the art of marketing was coming into its own, with businesses large and small realizing that the customer really does come first and excellence can be a way of life. Frankly, the thought of doing the book was intriguing, but I wondered whether I could do it, let alone find the time. The idea became feasible when I decided to retire from IBM two years earlier than planned. (As you may know, IBM has a policy wherein key officers are required to relinquish their positions at age sixty.) I was spending a considerable amount of time and energy in outside speaking engagements as part of my job as vice-president of marketing. So why not do two things? Write a book and start a new career on the lecture circuit.

However, the catalyst of my decision to write this book was Bob Shook, whom I met in 1979 when he was writing *The Ten Greatest Salespersons*, in which I

17

was included. Through Bob's initiative and my family's encouragement, I decided to go ahead. As an accomplished writer, he was invaluable in coordinating *The IBM Way*.

One other person who worked closely with me during the final manuscript preparation was my daughter Christy. She was a constructive critic and a significant editorial contributor.

Again, my main thrust was to convey the beliefs and values of IBM, since these principles had such a profound effect on my life, as well as to describe for the first time the specific details of how IBM markets. Sure, there has been some sensitivity about describing IBM's marketing, in light of the tough competitive marketplace that exists today. However, I have discussed our tactics and strategies hundreds of times in public over the years and know that the real difference is in the execution.

I wish there were some way to thank individually the literally thousands of IBMers who played an important role in my career. I can only hope that this book will in some way be a tribute to their great skills and valued friendships.

Also, I thank my parents, Harry and Hazel, for instilling in me a sense of integrity and a desire to do what's right.

The following people were interviewed for this book and contributed meaningful insights into the world of IBM: Dale Antonik, Stan Barchan, Dean Beckwith, Harry Bernhard, Ed Bullard, Conie DeLoca, Bob Erwin, Bob Evans, Chuck Francis, Steve Haeckel, Jack Hammond, David Hendrickson, Dick Kirkley, Don Laidlaw, Stan McElroy, Doug McMillan, David Miller, Jim O'Connell, Pete Schavoir, Bob Siegel.

SPECIAL
ACKNOWLEDGMENT

Irv Levey, as editor of this book, was a practitioner of excellence. He was the creative force in the rewriting of the manuscript. Any success the book may have will be a reflection of his dedicated efforts.

Introduction

There really *is* an IBM way of marketing and managing. Like the title of this book, IBM's approach to business, technology and people has nothing clever or slick about it. *How* it functions, and *why*, have more to do with IBM's success than *what* it does. Because that's true, all of the traits and characteristics that make IBM great can be emulated by any company of any size. I don't think a company or a business person anywhere can fail to learn something worthwhile from IBM.

Since we in the United States became self-conscious about the downward trend of productivity in our country, and the need to improve quality, scores of business books have been written. Some have been scholarly examinations of what's wrong with American companies and what's right with their Japanese competitors. They analyze and dissect, turn us inside out and leave us bloody on the operating table. Some show us how easy it is to climb the corporate ladder. Others reveal how to become rich and powerful, with the emphasis on looking out for number one. Still others concentrate on management theory and a fast-paced approach to becoming a more effective manager.

Every now and then – about as often as Halley's Comet streaks across the sky – a book like *In Search of Excellence* comes along and gets right to the heart of things. Without award-winning prose or mind-dulling jargon, it deals with failure by elucidating success, simply but not simplistically.

21

So why a book about IBM? For one thing, this $50 billion American company, which now employs 400,000 people and is the most profitable business in the world, is poised to double its revenues by the end of the decade. What makes this phenomenal growth possible, and what forces drive the company, are important, because what IBM does and how it does it have a tremendous impact on the business community and on society at large. Millions of people are directly affected by this company's activities.

To understand IBM's success and its unshakable optimism, one needs some insights into its marketing systems and philosophy, and its unique relationship with employees and customers. That's where I can be helpful. I know IBM from the inside out. For the past dozen or so years, I've been invited to speak with representatives of every type of business imaginable; and since my early retirement, I've not only increased my speaking engagements but also acted as consultant for some of the world's finest companies. They want to know how IBM does it. They're as fascinated by this company's amazing ability to roll with the punches, to change and adjust, as they are by its spectacular growth. I'm in demand because I know why IBM has the most highly motivated and productive marketing organization anywhere. Even the most successful companies want to know how an organization of such high achievers was put together and managed. They want to know how it's possible to sustain its level of excellence, year after year.

Among other things, *The IBM Way* will explain what it means to be a customer-driven organization; how IBM's marketing and sales orientation permeates every aspect of its operation; how its profound concern

22

for the customer goes far beyond guaranteeing satisfaction; how the IBM 'personality' is shaped by the company's insatiable quest for excellence.

This is the first book ever written about IBM by an IBM officer. A quick sketch of my IBM career will give you an idea of the depth of my involvement with the company, especially my connection with their sales and marketing operations:

Like almost everyone who ever held a managerial or an executive position at IBM, I started as a trainee and moved up through the ranks. I was a marketing rep who sold everything from electric typewriters to stored program systems; a special rep responsible for installing one of the very first large-scale computer systems; an administrative assistant to the executive vice-president, who was responsible for all IBM engineering, manufacturing, marketing and financial functions; a branch manager; the head of IBM's banking, finance, and brokerage business; Eastern Regional Sales Manager, responsible for more than a hundred branch offices; general manager for the Western Region; and president of the Data Processing Division, the US marketing operation for all IBM computer products. Then, finally, I became the company's chief marketing strategist, vice-president of marketing, with worldwide responsibility. That was my job for the past ten years. I now serve on five corporate boards of directors and four university advisory councils, and I lecture on eight university campuses each year. Activities such as these provide insight into the world outside IBM, as they broaden personal perspectives.

I'm a marketing person. A salesman. I've been referred to as a 'salesman's salesman', and I consider that the greatest compliment. Marketing and sales are so tightly woven into IBM's past, present, and future successes that they are inseparable.

Although I was part of the IBM marketing operation for thirty-four years, and responsible for that function for ten years, this is not going to be a book on management theory. Nor will it be a company history, and it sure won't be a kiss-and-tell book. Even if I hadn't been a satisfied employee and an admirer of this awesome giant, I wouldn't write a book to satisfy the gossip collector's appetite. It's not my style.

I have made two absolutely right decisions in my life: the first was to marry Helen; the second, to join IBM in 1950. While at IBM, I was offered the opportunity of becoming CEO of a variety of companies, including many in the computer industry. Though the offers were attractive, I was always challenged by my IBM assignments and remained a born-and-bred, dyed-in-the-wool IBMer.

The IBM Way will expose the heart and soul of IBM: how it thinks and behaves behind closed doors; what goes into its decisionmaking; what it deems important and how it stacks its priorities; why the great majority of its employees, recruited right out of college, never leave the company; why IBM's hundreds of thousands of employees never had a union; what kind of people become members of our army of blue-suiters; what's the truth about the much-talked-about dress code and relocation policy. Mostly, you'll get a good look into IBM's sales and marketing operation. I'll talk about everything that makes IBM IBM.

If because of this book other companies increase their level of productivity and profit, we all will benefit. And if competitors improve their operation and make an effort to close the gap, IBM will feel the heat and enjoy the challenge.

1

A Business and its Beliefs

The only sacred cow in an organization is its principles.

With more than 400,000 employees, annual sales that exceed $50 billion, and offices in almost every country in the world, IBM can be mind-boggling in its vastness, fascinating in its accomplishments. But to appreciate this business phenomenon, you must understand its corporate attitudes, feelings and behavior. Some people may have difficulty imagining that a corporation the size of IBM has humanistic characteristics, but it does. And I'm convinced that it's these very human qualities that are responsible for IBM's incredible success.

I don't know how many companies have actually had a code of behavior articulated for them, but that's what Thomas J. Watson, Sr, did for IBM when he founded it in 1914. Like any ambitious entrepreneur, he wanted his company to be financially successful, but he also wanted it to reflect some of his personal values. These values, which he put down on paper, became the foundation for his new company; and anyone who worked for him thereafter knew exactly what Tom, Sr's, company was all about.

Watson's tenets, which were reaffirmed by his son, Thomas Watson, Jr, in 1956, when he became IBM's second CEO, are uncomplicated and can be easily understood by everyone from the CEO's office to the mailroom. They are:

1. The individual must be respected.
2. The customer must be given the best possible service.
3. Excellence and superior performance must be pursued.

These commitments, which remain at the heart of the company's operation, are so revered and encompassing that every action and policy is directly influenced by them. I think that anyone who studies the development of IBM will agree that Watson's philosophy has more to do with the company's success than do its technological innovations, marketing skills or financial resources. IBM doesn't have a patent on corporate values, principles and philosophies. However, I don't think any company can become great without them. Principles, though, can quickly become empty slogans. They're like muscles that turn soft and weak if they're not exercised regularly. To be important in a business environment, principles must first be articulated to every employee, repeated so often that everyone understands just how seriously they are to be taken. IBM conscientiously drives home its philosophical messages at meetings, in internal publications and memos, at company gatherings and in private conversations. None of this would mean anything, of course, if IBM's management did not demonstrate, by personal deeds and actions, what these beliefs mean. It requires diligence, but it works. Employees understand that not only the company's success is dependent upon their faithful adherence to Tom Watson's principles, but so

is their personal success. And that means a
employees. It takes time, but once your peop
you, every facet of your business is positively affected.

The First Commitment

The individual must be respected. No one can be
against this. At least, no one would admit it.

After all, respecting the rights and dignity of the
individual has been advocated by many cultures and
religions throughout history. But while almost everybody agrees with the idea, seldom is it found in the
doctrine of a business, let alone practiced. Of course,
IBM isn't the only company that advocates this, but
not enough companies do.

Far too many employers abuse their employees.
They may demean them by overtly outrageous actions
or they may chip away at their self-esteem subtly and
covertly; often, they look the other way while their
supervisors and managers do the dirty work. Such
behavior bothered Tom Watson, Sr, as it bothers some
of us today. He couldn't solve the problem universally,
but he could do something about it in his own company. He truly wanted the people who worked for him
to feel good about themselves and their work. No one
could be paid enough money to be compensated for
being made uncomfortable and unhappy by his
supervisors.

Tom, Sr, was particularly intent on building the self-
respect and self-confidence of his marketing reps. For
years, when he was a salesman in the field, he may
have suffered from low esteem. Those were the days of

the 'drummer', and selling was not a respected career – especially traveling salesman.

He said, 'I want the IBM salesmen to be looked up to. Admired. I want their wives and children to be proud of them. I don't want their mothers to feel that they have to apologize for them when asked what their sons are doing.'

His early emphasis on human relations was not motivated by altruism alone, but as Tom Watson, Jr, put it, 'by the simple belief that if we respected our people and helped them respect themselves, the company would certainly profit.'

The Watsons understood that people, not money or things, are a company's greatest asset. Ever since IBM's earliest days, an ongoing campaign has stressed that *each individual makes a difference.* So that nobody feels like a number, the company tries to create a small-business atmosphere. Branch offices are kept small, and the company is pretty successful at maintaining a one-to-twelve manager-to-employee ratio. All managers understand the value of job satisfaction, and the need to motivate their people continually. Superior performances are rewarded by recognition, promotions and money. Compensation will be discussed fully in a later chapter, but I'll say here that there are no automatic raises for IBMers, no cost-of-living increases – and it's possible for a fairly new marketing rep to earn more than one who has been with the company for many years. Each person gets paid on the basis of what he produces, not on his longevity. Those who do exceptionally well are paid accordingly.

Since IBM opened its doors, the company has had a full-employment tradition. This is as true today, with nearly 400,000 employees, as it was when there were only hundreds of people in the company. An employee who produces always has an assignment, preferably a meaningful one. In nearly fifty years, no person employed on a regular basis has lost as much as one hour of working time because of a layoff. Like all businesses, IBM has had its share of difficult times. It has taken careful planning and commitment to maintain full employment. Perhaps the most dramatic way to help achieve this is through retraining, which often requires career changes and/or relocation. For example, during the economically troubled years 1969–72, more than twelve thousand IBM employees moved from plants, labs and headquarters with light workloads to locations where they were needed. More than five thousand employees were retrained for new careers in sales, customer engineering, field administration and programming. Most ended up with comparable or better jobs.

Again, in 1975, during the severe recession, nearly 3,800 employees were placed in new positions to balance a workload. It cost a lot of money, but it was important. This doesn't mean the company is benevolent and paternalistic to the degree that nobody has ever been terminated. People are dismissed for poor performance, usually early in their career. IBM couldn't afford to spend so much to reward the good performers if it had to subsidize those who do not produce.

Productive people need challenging assignments. It's vital for them to go home at night feeling that they did something worthwhile. And when they enjoy their work and know the company cares about them, they want to contribute to its growth.

IBM's practice is to promote people from within. In

all my years with the company, I recall only three executives – all in highly specialized fields – who were brought in from the outside. Everyone knows that if he works hard and aspires to a higher position, he will have an opportunity to advance. It's frustrating and demoralizing for an ambitious person to work his tail off, striving for a certain job, only to have someone from the outside come in and get it. I know the argument that promoting only from within can lead to inbreeding, but I don't accept it. The negative effect that bringing in outsiders has on morale far outweighs the hazards of inbreeding.

IBM has many programs to let a person know he or she can make a difference, and I'll discuss a few of them later. But there is a host of little things that you might notice at IBM headquarters in Armonk, New York. For instance, there are no titles on any doors or desks, no bathrooms designed for 'executive use only', no reserved parking spaces, no executive dining room. All in all, it's a very democratic environment, where everyone is treated with the same respect. Even IBM's equal opportunity policy and affirmative action programs go far beyond government guidelines. In fact, the company's minority population equals or exceeds the minority percentage mix of the US population.

IBM strives to be a responsible corporate citizen. From a dollar perspective, the company's 1984 contributions to social, cultural and educational programs exceeded $145 million. IBM's attitude toward the individual extends far beyond company headquarters. Management treats everyone who works at IBM with respect and, in turn, expects everyone to treat customers, suppliers and even the competition the same way. The company's code of conduct states that no

IBMer shall disparage any competitor; that selling must be done on the merits of products and services: sell strengths and never try to exploit someone else's weaknesses. The code also advises not to boast about the company's size, success or position in the industry; or about how much is spent on research and product development; or about how many systems engineers there are to work with customers. It's all right to talk about the *quality* of IBM's products or services, the resources and people that represent a commitment to the customer and the concept of excellence. It's OK for a rep to tell the customer about an IBM educational facility that is staffed and equipped to give him the best possible service. That's not boasting of bigness; it's a fact and it's relevant to the customer's needs.

The Watsons believed that when one respects the individual one shows consideration of *all* people – in and out of the company. And that belief must be reinforced constantly by one's actions.

The first time I met Tom Watson, Jr, I quickly learned that he practiced what he preached. I was new to the company and completing the final sales training program at the sales school in Poughkeepsie, New York. Although I was happy and excited about getting an opportunity to work for IBM, I was at the same time under considerable personal strain. My wife was pregnant and expecting to deliver at any moment. Though we had agreed that I must complete this initial phase of my training, no matter what, I was having second thoughts. I wanted to be with Helen, but I was afraid to ask for the time off – especially since I didn't know exactly when the baby would be born. It could be happening right now, it could be tomorrow or next week – or longer.

Watson spoke to the class, and when he was finished he moved around the room, chatting with the trainees. I was wondering if I had time to call home, when he approached me.

'How are things going? What's happening?'

Well, he asked so I told him. I hadn't got the words out of my mouth when he interrupted.

'What are you doing here? You should be home with your wife. Get on a plane and get back to Ohio immediately.'

Within the next few minutes, IBM's CEO made arrangements for this trainee to get to Cleveland, and I was airborne that same afternoon.

In the lectures, I heard a lot about respect for the individual, but the message was made crystal clear when Watson demonstrated how he placed my family and my personal worth above the business.

Among the flowers that were delivered to the hospital room after the arrival of my daughter was a beautiful arrangement from Tom Watson.

'Do we know him?' Helen asked.

In 1969, I wrote to the twenty-eight thousand people in my division:

Respect for the individual is not a platitude. It is a constant in IBM, the initial belief on which our business was founded. Its effectiveness depends entirely on the extent to which it is encouraged by every manager in this company, and practiced by every employee.

But respect for the individual can become a platitude, if it is not continually reemphasized and

—

consciously made a part of our day-to-day business relationships.

The dramatic changes of our business increase rather than diminish our need to respect one another.

The Second Commitment

Customer Service. When Tom Watson, Sr, said that he wanted IBM to provide *the best service in the world*, he referred to service by any company, not just in his own industry. To accomplish this, he mandated that IBM would be a *customer-oriented company*. That is, every part of its operation would focus on the customers' requirements. Every employee's job description is somehow related to IBM's goal of providing customers, prospects and vendors with the best possible service.

It's a shame, but in America today when we get good service we are surprised by it. People don't expect it, they don't demand it, and they settle for a lot less than they should. When customers are first exposed to IBM's brand of service, they are usually taken aback. But it's easy to get used to the kind of treatment that makes you feel important. And every customer with every company should be made to feel that way.

To let the customer know how important he is, IBM tries to respond to, if not resolve, any complaint within twenty-four hours of its receipt. When a customer requests a service call, the response is even quicker – frequently within the hour. Similarly, IBM has introduced more efficient ways of providing service to its customers. IBM specialists are available via toll-free numbers to solve service and software problems over the phone. Lower-priced carry-in and mail-in service agreements have been added to give customers a wider range of choices. In addition, IBM has established guidelines requiring that each new IBM product be superior in quality to the one it replaces, and to comparable products in the marketplace. IBM strives to provide its customers with superior products and service.

The quality of its service depends upon an organization's training and educational capabilities. In this area, IBM believes that it has made the largest financial commitment of any company in the world. Its training and educational programs are unparalleled in business. The hours logged in the classroom are believed to exceed those spent in any major university. Each year, every IBM manager is given forty hours of training, and that extends down through the organization. Even customers are routinely invited to participate in a variety of classroom programs. In an industry where repeat business is essential for long-term growth, it is essential to make sure that the initial order is only the beginning. Outstanding service is what keeps bringing the customer back to do more business.

The Third Commitment

Watson's third mandate is *excellence* – the pursuit of all tasks with the idea that they can be accomplished in a superior fashion. The constant goal is zero defects, in product and service. Though Watson of course knew that perfection is never possible, to aim for less would lower expectations and weaken his program. In its striving for the impossible, the company established certain satisfaction indexes so it could regularly sample the marketplace to establish the quality of its service. More about that later.

Excellence begins with the recruiting program. IBM believes that the best students selected from the nation's best colleges may be the most responsive to the company's intensive training program and the most highly motivated to do superior work. So a lot more is involved than simply attracting the outstanding young people. To achieve excellence, they need superior training and must feel compelled to succeed. At IBM, a highly competitive environment creates an atmosphere that nurtures excellence. Needless to say, a great deal of peer pressure exists. Nobody owns a job at IBM. With the intensity of competition and the continual emphasis on education, there's no room for individual complacency. The insistence on peak performance sets a rigid pace. People begin to think that anything can be achieved – that anything is possible. That attitude generates excitement. You feel it in the air.

When an organization demands and gets excellence from its people, the excitement eventually becomes contagious. Its customers, too, become optimistic and enthusiastic, and think: 'This is the kind of organization I want to do business with.'

The Only Sacred Cow

Tom Watson, Jr, said: 'For any organization to survive and achieve success, there must be a sound set of principles on which it bases all of its policies and actions. But more important is its faithful adherence to those principles.' Does Watson's credo hold up in times of change?

In business, everything about an organization's operation is subject to change. Locations change. People change. Products change. (IBM originally manufactured butcher scales and time clocks.) Names change. (Until 1924, IBM was known as the Computing-Tabulating-Recording Company.) We live in a world of constant change, and in business, one's survival is dependent upon a capacity to change. (In the 1950s, I was involved with the installation of the largest and most expensive system of its time, the 705 computer. It had a price tag of approximately $1,500,000 and took up an entire room. Today, the three-thousand-dollar Personal Computer that sits on my desktop at home has more capacity than the 705!) In an era of high technology, change is both frequent and swift. Marketing programs that don't respond to the changes can destroy a company. You either go forward or go backward; you can't stand still.

The only sacred cow in an organization is its principles. A company must never change them. No matter what its nature or size, there must be certain bedrock beliefs to serve as its guiding force. While a company must be flexible, always regrouping and changing with the times, its beliefs must remain irrevocable, deeply embedded throughout time. IBM's three basic beliefs are so fundamental to success that any deviation is unthinkable.

I wish that every business would establish a set of principles to serve as a guide for its people. Although the best time to do it is upon starting a business, few fledgling entrepreneurs think in such terms. They are too busy making a living to formulate principles that will guide them in what seems the distant future. However, at some point their philosophies should be recorded; and once formulated, they should not be kept a secret, but be loud and clear to everyone.

When a business is small, its owner generally has personal contact with his key people and conveys his convictions on a one-to-one basis. If he doesn't discuss his philosophy with his employees, he certainly demonstrates it by example. As an organization grows and prospers, it must make sure every level of management understands and practices the same established principles. For the most part, if you study outstanding American organizations that have weathered the test of time, you will find well-articulated philosophies behind their behavior. The success of a business is measured in more than dollars and cents. As Al Williams, a former IBM president, said: 'It is not bigness we seek, it is greatness. Bigness is imposing. Greatness is enduring.'

An organization must constantly communicate its beliefs to its people. At the onset of the IBM training program, new people are introduced to the philosophy of the company, along with its history and tradition. However, it's one thing to talk about beliefs and values, and quite another to incorporate them into the very fabric of your organization. An Emerson quote comes to mind: 'What you are ... thunders, for I cannot hear what you say.' Actions, tactics, strategies, implementation, inspection, measurement, recognition and commitment – those are what's important. Not just words. I believe In Search of Excellence, by Tom Peters and Bob Waterman, was so successful because it struck a nerve in America: not because it told us anything new, but because it confirmed that which we already understood. It reaffirmed that paying attention to detail, doing things right the first time, practicing good human relations and being market-driven separate the leading organizations from the rest.

IBM marketing trainees see the company's code of behavior at work, in the office and in the field, during their very first week on the payroll. They learn what IBM means by respect for the individual. They see how they're personally treated. Nobody is ever too busy to help them with a problem. They see how customers are treated, and hear the praise given to the helpful marketing reps, systems engineers and service reps. They're surrounded by people striving for excellence. Soon, what appeared to be rhetoric becomes reality. Examples of the IBM beliefs are printed regularly in many company publications, and reports of outstanding service are repeated in classrooms, at branch office meetings and customer conferences. A major effort is constantly at work to keep the company's ideals alive, healthy and valued.

The three tenets – respect, service and excellence – are as important to IBM today as when first uttered by Thomas Watson, Sr, in 1914. The Watsons didn't simply communicate a set of principles to hear themselves say something nice. They lived by their beliefs in their day-to-day work.

To me, Tom, Jr, was a great man – but he wasn't perfect. He had a pretty good temper and could be impatient with what he thought to be inconsiderate behavior. When I was president of the Data Processing Division, he sent a message to my office asking that I come to a meeting at three o'clock that same afternoon. It was a special session, with little advance notice, and I was already on my way to New Jersey to see a customer. Arriving at the customer's office, I received a call from my secretary: Watson had called a meeting and wanted me there. The customer situation was a difficult one, and I didn't get back to Armonk until six-thirty that evening. As an object lesson, Watson hadn't started the meeting, so everyone was waiting for me. Now, as much as I admired the man, I didn't want to be on the receiving end of his wrath, and I assumed that he was building up a pretty good head of steam.

As I walked into the room, he said, 'When I call for a three o'clock meeting, I expect *everybody* to be there at three o'clock.'

I took a deep breath. 'Tom, how many times have you said, "The customer comes first"? I was with one in New Jersey who had a very serious problem.'

Watson's face softened. 'Buck,' he said, smiling, 'you have the right priorities.'

There was a brief pause; he turned to the others and said, 'We shall now commence the meeting.'

As IBM prospered over the years, both Watsons showed an enormous amount of flexibility in responding to the changing times. But neither would ever bend or compromise the basic values that are at the heart of the company's very existence. Nor would I.

2

Leadership

---

*A real leader has the ability to motivate others to
their highest level of achievement; then gives them
the opportunity and the freedom to grow.*

The Watsons were role models for just about everyone
who ever climbed IBM's organizational ladder. I was
no exception. It was easy for me to incorporate their
business values into my own style of leadership, which
often differed from but never seriously conflicted with
theirs. It was easy because I truly believed in their
approach to people and problems.

Fortunately for me, the Watsons provided a nurturing environment that allowed me to develop. They
considered my success their success.

Too many people work under insecure leaders,
whose paranoia stifles the growth of everyone around
them. A leader who runs scared fills the environment
with tension, hostility and tentativeness. He batters
the self-esteem of his people, frightening them just as
he is frightened. He kills incentive in the very people
he must motivate in order to achieve his prescribed
goals. This kind of manager can cripple an organization, and is a leader in rank only.

I promise not to fill this chapter with sports analogies, but you can certainly see a variety of leadership
styles, on any weekend, by switching your TV dial

from one sports event to another – from Indiana's explosive Bobby Knight to Dallas's cool Tom Landry.

Regardless of his style, *a real leader, through his or her actions and words, has the ability to motivate others to their highest level of achievement; then gives them the opportunity and the freedom to grow.*

In this chapter, I'll tell you what I think it takes to be a good leader; how I led a marketing group that numbered tens of thousands of bright, ambitious people; and which of my characteristics helped me get the job done.

I've received a lot of recognition for my work at IBM, in and out of the house. Today, major corporations everywhere pay me handsome fees to address their top management conferences. I've been asked so many questions about my own style of leadership that I've been forced to analyze it.

Here are some personal traits that affected the way I manage, and have helped me become successful:

1. *I like people.* I like them better than computers, sports or books. I love to talk and I like to listen, and couldn't imagine working in a position that isolated me from others.

2. *I feel good about myself.* I'm comfortable with my values and my personal philosophy. Whenever I consider doing anything that conflicts with those values, warning lights flash in my brain and I reevaluate and rethink my motives.

3. *For me, to be given responsibility is an honor.* I know that the greater the responsibility, the greater the challenge. The greater the risk, the greater the reward. Although I've made my living for more than thirty years as a motivator, and know how important

'incentives' are, I've always been more motivated by the challenge of responsibility than by the promise of financial gain. Of course, I've never turned down any money that IBM offered, but I don't think it was the money that made me perk. On the other hand, I might have developed a different attitude if IBM had been less generous.

4. *I like to solve problems, and believe that any problem that can be uncovered and articulated can be solved.* A trouble-free position would bore me.

5. *My temperament is such that I don't have to win every point to have been in a successful debate.*

You can see that I believe a successful leader must have a good sense of self-worth and purpose.

The Siamese Twins

You can't talk about leadership without talking about responsibility and accountability; as far as I'm concerned, you can't separate the two. A leader must delegate responsibility and provide the freedom to make decisions, and then be held accountable for the results. It seems simple enough, but leadership often runs into roadblocks right from the outset. Frequently it's the fault of the person who delegates. That's because he does it with his fingers crossed. He goes through the ritual of delegating but he just can't let go. Perhaps he has second thoughts about the decision, or maybe he's afraid that he's weakened his own power base. Whatever the reason, he intends to keep an eye on things. Soon he is breathing down the neck of his newly appointed manager, scrutinizing every action, criticizing every decision, allowing little or no room for expression or experiment. He renders his manager helpless and then holds him accountable for the results. The poor guy doesn't have a chance. He stops trying to be innovative, and by not exercising his authority, returns the decisionmaking to his boss. He becomes an implementer, which is probably what he was before his promotion. The people who work under this manager know that he's powerless – and they resent it. They want to work for a winner. His promotion may have added something to his paycheck, but it can never be enough for what it cost him in self-esteem and peace of mind. He was a victim of the 'captain of the ship' syndrome, in which the person at the top assumes all the responsibility.

There are times when the opposite occurs. A person is given the responsibility, authority and freedom to get a job done, but is never held accountable. A business can be driven into the ground because a leader recklessly delegates responsibility as if he were getting rid of a hot potato, then detaches himself from the delegate and his decisions. It catches up with him eventually, when a crisis surfaces that he can't avoid. This kind of leader doesn't want to be held accountable, but somehow doesn't hold the other person accountable either. It seems impossible, doesn't it? But it happens somewhere every day. Personally, I want to be held accountable and responsible for whatever decisions I have the freedom and authority to make and to implement.

Implementing Someone Else's Decisions

There are times when a person in a leadership position has to implement a decision that he didn't make and may not completely agree with. At one time or another, everyone in management is involved in a frustrating or unpopular decision: maybe a budget cut, or the scrapping of a project or product. More than once in my career I found myself in that position, and I have firm beliefs about what a strong leader must do in such a situation.

If I was part of the decisionmaking process, I would certainly argue my point of view. Until the decision was reached, I'd do everything possible to swing the others involved to my way of thinking. But once the decision was made, even though my point of view did not prevail, I would treat that decision as if it were my own. Furthermore, I would implement it with the same interest and enthusiasm as if it were. Sometimes that's difficult, especially if it turns out to be an unpopular decision. But for a strong leader it's imperative. Besides, what about the times when the shoe is on the other foot, and my decision has to be implemented by people who may have opposed it?

In situations like this, weak leaders go to their people and say, 'Look, this decision comes from top management. I don't like it any more than you do. Believe me, I tried to shoot it down but failed. Now we're stuck with it, and it's up to us to make it work.'

He apologizes for the decision! He separates himself from management. He says, 'Hey, I'm not one of them, I'm one of you.'

By encouraging a 'we-they' attitude, he hurts the

company, causes dissatisfaction and unrest, and most of all, demeans himself as a manager and a leader. He thinks that he's strengthening his position with the troops. He's wrong! He's presenting the decisionmaking process as a confrontation in which there are winners and losers; he's telling his people, loud and clear, that he's a loser. He's also demonstrating that when some people don't get their way, they bad-mouth those who do.

Well, such a leader certainly undermines his staff's perception of his effectiveness. When a person in a leadership position separates himself from the decisionmakers, his people take notice and begin to question his ability to manage. The change in their attitude toward him may be so subtle that he does not see it happening, but once he puts himself on the sidelines he is no longer taken seriously.

These so-called leaders would not be part of my team for long – not the dictator who can't delegate responsibility, or the procrastinator who avoids making a decision. None of my people could flip-flop in and out of management and survive. These types weaken the managerial structure of a company. They are usually a major source of rumors and gossip. They confuse the people in their department and, as they try to be on the popular side of any company issue, more often than not add fuel to any smoldering fire.

Although I believe that a good manager carries out the decisions of his superiors as though they were his own, I'm not advocating blind allegiance. Every person should know, and set, his limits. If what you're expected to implement is contrary to your basic values, you must resolve it to your satisfaction, one way or another – but never by underhandedly trying to sabotage the decision.

I have said that I consider it my responsibility to argue my point of view in the decisionmaking process. That is true, but I'm a pragmatist who carefully picks and chooses the fights I get involved in. I'm not interested in winning a battle if I end up losing the war. We all know people who fight for every point as if their life depended on it. They get a reputation for being argumentative, hardheaded and unreasonable. After a while you can't tell which points are important to them and which aren't. Before long, this kind of person is left out of the decisionmaking process whenever possible – and isn't taken too seriously when he can't be avoided.

Setting Priorities

A good manager and leader has to be able to set priorities, not only in the battles he opts to get into, but in just about everything he does. So let's talk about priorities.

In a large corporation, priorities have to be set at every level. The corporate goals have a tremendous impact on the priorities of everyone in management. At IBM, how those goals are to be achieved affect the priorities of everyone in all functions – engineering, manufacturing, marketing, etc. I can visualize a company's priorities as a set of boxes that nestle, one into another – starting with a large box, symbolizing the corporate priorities, and ending with a small box, which might symbolize the papers piled up in each individual's in box. A good leader has to be the master of his own box. He has to know how to prioritize its contents or he'll be buried in details, wondering where the time went and why so little was accomplished. I've known people who immerse themselves in minutiae, sometimes giving to a routine memo, which requires only a minimal response, the same time and attention they devote to a more serious matter. Some people hide in their in box. It's a way for them to put off dealing with things that may be difficult but should have a high priority.

The best managers know how to stack their priorities, quickly and with certainty, and do not get caught up in details that erode their time and managerial effectiveness.

There are so many options today, so much to choose from, that one must constantly sort out things one needs from those one wants or yearns for. Too many managers have an insatiable desire for more people, more money, more resources. Necessity versus desirability is a frequent conflict. Too often desire wins out – usually at the company's expense. An executive who gives in to desire may put too much fat into his head count or spend too much of his budget on nonessential programs. You must be able to make a clear distinction between what is desirable and what is necessary.

Priorities – they are a continuous consideration. Do you build on your strengths or do you struggle to improve your weaknesses? Do you invest in a training program so that you can promote from within, or do you spend the money for higher-priced outside talent? Good leaders constantly think in terms of priorities. They pick and choose, and are aware of the impact of each decision. They also keep assessing their ordering of things and carefully restack them if necessary. One thing is sure: if most of your time is spent on items that are not very high on your list of priorities, you're headed for trouble.

I must say this for IBM: regardless of its size and complex structure, its leaders have never been bureaucratic paper shufflers. They try to keep things simple and paperwork at a minimum.

I decided a long time ago that if I was to be a really topnotch manager, I'd have to limit the number of things that I could get deeply involved in. Somewhere along the way, I set the limit at five. Five objectives, five items on my list of priorities; and I insisted that the people who worked for me also limited their objectives to five. The problem rarely was getting them to stretch to five – rather it was inducing them to cut back on objectives. That doesn't mean I didn't permit myself or them to be involved in more than five things. Simply, we were expected to devote most of our time and energy to the five most important things on the agenda. The upside of this is obvious. There was less shifting of gears, fewer distractions. The most important things got done more efficiently and more quickly. You need your priorities, all right, but you can't have such a long list of them that you spread yourself too thin.

There was a downside to limiting myself to five major areas of interest, but it was minimal. When I narrowed the focus of my attention, I became less of an authority about things on the periphery, or outside my primary interests. At first it bothered me. I thought that people expected me to have an answer to almost any question right on the tip of my tongue, and I didn't like disappointing them. But it didn't take long for me to come up with an acceptable response:

'I don't know, but I'll find out and get back to you.' What made it acceptable was my never failing to follow up. No one had to ask me twice. This approach is a lot better than 'hip shooting' an answer and then wishing you hadn't responded so fast.

Having Integrity

If you're to be a successful leader you must have integrity. People must know what to expect from you. Once you make a commitment to a person or a task, you must honour it. I try to live by that, down to the smallest detail. I return phone calls promptly; I answer letters; I meet deadlines. I work at doing things right the first time, and everybody knows it. To me, there's no greater compliment than for people to say, 'I can always count on Buck Rodgers.' It's a matter of living up to my word, time after time. And since the people I work with can count on me, I feel that I have every right to expect as much from them.

From the time I was a marketing rep, I established myself as dependable, especially where my customers were concerned. I did that by never making a promise I couldn't keep. It wasn't always easy. I remember rough times in the mid-sixties when we were having some difficult production problems. To guarantee a specific delivery date wasn't always possible, and often the sale hinged on that issue. It was tempting to come up with a date that would satisfy the customer, figuring that you'd dance around the problem when the disappointed customer confronted you. But I never 'danced'. It was more difficult to sell, but I made a special effort to be totally realistic with each customer, never misleading him about our ability to deliver. It may sound corny, but I was determined to establish the fact that my word was my bond. I could never do business any other way – and I'm lucky that I worked for a company that never attempted to put a strain on that value. As a rep, I felt that I was IBM's front man. What the customer would think about me, he would think about IBM. As the president of a large division, and then an officer of the company, I felt the same way – not only about the customer but also about the thousands of IBMers for whom I represented top management.

I said earlier that a good leader is a motivator, one who inspires superior performance by his actions and words. I had my role models at IBM. Among them were Vincent Learson, Frank Cary and L. H. (Red) La Motte. Learson followed Tom Watson, Jr., as CEO. He was tough and demanding, but fair. Cary, his successor, was a master strategist, who at the same time encouraged creative thinking. La Motte, executive vice-president during the Watson era, was a great people motivator, who proved that nice guys can finish first. Just as these men were my role models, I consciously tried to be one for others.

A good role model is almost always a good performer. He does his job so well that it's obvious to the people he works with. He treats his position with respect and his mission or goals with commitment. I don't mean that he exudes solemn staidness and gets carried away with himself – I do mean that he doesn't belittle the importance of his position, his work or the goals he's expected to achieve.

Every time I took a new assignment at IBM, I received what we called a mission statement; some companies call them job descriptions. I'd study these statements and then I'd throw them away. I wasn't being rebellious, but I knew that I couldn't possibly do everything covered in the statement. I felt I had to decide just what was necessary to accomplish the goals set forth, and which of my experiences and skills would help me get the job done. I never believed in trying to press a person into a mold I designed for him. For myself, I wanted to help create the positions to which I was assigned, and I wanted the same for the people who were my responsibility. I wanted them to treat their mission statements as I did: as guidelines.

Energizing the Environment

I love to work. I'm an enthusiastic person by nature, and so it's with great enthusiasm that I approach every assignment. I considered it my responsibility to charge the atmosphere with excitement and optimism. I was fully aware that the attitude of any leader, positive or negative, which characterizes his style, rubs off on the people he works with. Unfortunately, too many people in leadership positions are terrible role models. They enervate rather than energize their people. An old adage says: 'Age may wrinkle the face, but lack of enthusiasm wrinkles the soul.' I believe that; but I think that lack of enthusiasm wrinkles the face too.

Still, I must caution you that a good leader's optimism must be realistic. Unfounded optimism can be as destructive as unfounded pessimism. For instance, they take great pains, at IBM, in setting attainable sales quotas for reps. Often it is necessary to stretch to bring in the forecasted sales, but the stretch is considered a realistic part of the projection. Plenty of companies announce sales quotas that are 30, 40, even 50 percent higher than they honestly expect to achieve. I consider that to be poor management at best, and possibly even deceptiveness.

I never wanted reps to go into the field feeling that the company had stacked the cards against them. Once they entered customers' offices, they had to project IBM's enthusiasm and mine. And a person can't do that if he thinks he's getting a raw deal. The blending of realism and optimism is the key to an upbeat selling season.

A Winning Attitude

A successful leader in marketing projects a winning attitude to his people, and through them to the customers they serve. You'll see what a high premium we put on winning when I discuss compensation and motivation later on. I've always admired the former professional football coach George Allen, who used to tell his players, 'Winning is living. Every time you win, you are reborn. Every time you lose, you die a little.' That may be excessive, but I agree that winning is an incredibly exhilarating experience, and losing is a bummer.

Because I'm a high-energy person and have a reputation for always striving for 'a little more', people who don't know me very well could get the idea that I'm a workaholic. They're wrong. I've known people who are proud to say that they reached the pinnacle of their profession by working sixteen or eighteen hours a day, six or seven days a week. They brag that they haven't had a vacation for years, and when they do take a day off, they call the office three or four times.

I'm not interested in judging other people, but I could never consider myself successful if I had to devote my life to my work. I said that I love to work, and I do. But somewhere along the line I developed the philosophy of working to live rather than living to work. When I'm on the job – in or out of the office – I give the task at hand my complete attention and concentration, and whatever energy is needed to get the job done. I pace myself. I don't want to run out of steam, physically or mentally. It bewilders me when managers demand 120 percent from their people, when I've never been able to give 100 percent of myself, except in short spurts. You really need to know when an extra effort is required, and that's when you must inspire people to reach back and draw upon their reserves. I've missed my share of dinners with my family and given up a few weekends to my work, but these were the exceptions. I never saw a correlation between hours worked and work accomplished that gave me any reason to believe the workaholic was the most productive kind of performer. It doesn't make sense to me that he would be. Most things done in excess are exhausting, and tired people cannot be the most efficient workers. But what really bothers me is what happens to the workaholic's field of vision, his interests and his personal relationships.

It's unfortunate when a family is sacrificed because a person can't work out a balance between work, family and play. A notably productive salesperson recently confided that he never had a meal with his family except on Sundays, never attended his children's graduations or watched them perform in a school event; he worked six days a week from 7 A.M. until 10 P.M. throughout his career – and considers himself to be one of the most successful salespeople in the world. Not in my book! I'm not condemning this workaholic. I feel sorry for him. It's too bad that a person has to give so much of himself, and his family and his freedom, to do a job that someone else could do just as well expending reasonable time and energy.

In my thirty-four years at IBM, I never shirked a responsibility or put out less than the job required. In fact, I always gave a little extra. I can say the same about my performance as a family man. I even manage to get in some time for myself. In addition to running five miles a day, I am a three-handicap golfer and an 'A' tennis player. That's not too shabby for a guy my age.

Balancing Act I

I advocate balance in one's life. Of course, you have to give a fair day's work for a fair day's pay. If your family and your sense of social responsibility and your value system aren't high, or if your compulsion to work drives everything else out of your life, then you've got a serious problem. Regarding social responsibility, I think we all have a 'civic rent' to pay during our lifetime. Happily, our society has moved from the 'me' generation to what I refer to as the 'be' generation. This means you can be anything you want to be, depending on your skills and capabilities. People want to *be* something; they want to contribute; they can't just be takers. What we choose to do is personal, whether it's working in a drug abuse program or for a charitable organization or toward getting band uniforms for the local school. Every good leader I know encourages his people to find ways to express themselves outside their work life. Not only do they and their community benefit; so does their company.

Recently, I was invited to speak to the top management of a multibillion-dollar manufacturer. The thrust of one of my messages was that every business person should get involved in civic activities, away from the business. The group seemed a little uneasy, and I sensed that I had hit a nerve. Later, in a private conversation, the chairman of the board told me that it wasn't unusual for the key people in the audience to work six or seven days a week. That was the pace he personally set – and demanded. It had been his style of management for many years, and his company was successful; but he agreed that perhaps there was a changing value system to be dealt with, and said that my ideas were worth considering. Shortly afterward, he invited me to serve as a consultant to his company. I was flattered, and pleased to accept.

Seeking Advice

Not only do I give advice when asked, I also never hesitate to seek it. Yet for some people I know, asking for advice is more difficult than asking for money. They somehow feel that it's a display of weakness, or that it makes them vulnerable to criticism. Well, I learned a long time ago that there are people much brighter than I, who at times have the ability to cut through a complex problem that has had me buffaloed. I also found that often the best advice comes from someone who brings to the table a totally different point of view. The most successful leaders feel comfortable asking for the advice of others whenever they need it. They make no attempt to project an image of an all-knowing, omnipotent executive. There are lots of good reasons to ask for advice, but high among them is that it's the greatest compliment you can give, demonstrating that you think enough of someone to involve him in a problem you have. Asking for advice should become part of every leader's repertoire of management techniques.

When you're in a highly structured organization, you may be inhibited from going for advice to someone below or above you on the organizational chart. Most people feel OK about asking their immediate supervisor or a peer for advice; but what about your boss's boss? Will you be stepping on someone's ego? Or what about going to someone two or three rungs down the ladder from you? Would that be considered a tactical error in your company? Frankly, I go to whoever I think can help me – whether it's for advice or for information. And that seems to work pretty well throughout IBM. I don't see any reason to stand on ceremony when you need help. You should know who has the expertise in your organization, and make use of it. I welcome anyone into my office, whatever his or her position in the company. I'm delighted when someone comes to me to find out what it takes to 'make it' at IBM. When an executive purports to have an 'open door policy' but people rarely take advantage of it, it's usually because he is sending out double messages – one being 'Don't take my invitation seriously'. Either that, or people are being discouraged from going over the heads of their managers.

Just as I've never been shy about asking for advice, I've never been afraid to surround myself with the best staff possible. It's one of the easiest ways to get a reputation for being a first-rate manager. The leader who selects his staff with the insight of a topnotch casting director is certain to have an easier time of it than the manager who defers to his personnel department. Everybody who's ever worked in a corporation has heard of the manager who is so insecure that he actually avoids hiring the best people. He is afraid that the 'new kid on the block' will show him up or somehow make him look bad, and eventually push him out of his job. It's another form of job paranoia, of running scared. I never thought in those terms. I always tried to find the best of the best, and when they met my expectations I saw to it that they advanced. If they chased after my job, so much the better. They performed at a higher level than they might have done otherwise.

Praising in Public, Criticizing in Private

Not everyone I hired performed as well as I had hoped. Even the best of them had occasional lapses of good judgment, just as I did and sometimes still do. When someone you give responsibility to doesn't live up to expectations as a leader, you are faced with one of your most difficult tasks – confronting the person and criticizing the performance. Some managers find it almost impossible to handle a confrontation with someone they are closely associated with. At times, they fail to do their own job properly by letting the mediocre or incorrect work slide by, with barely a mention. On the other hand, I've seen managers who seem to delight in chewing out an employee – often in front of his co-workers. I can understand, but not tolerate, the manager who wants to avoid a scene, and I have no respect at all for the tyrant. I don't think anyone should be humiliated or demeaned because of his errors or bad judgements. Nor should a leader allow the quality of work to become low because he's too weak to demand that it remain high.

I think that at one time I was perceived as an easygoing type of manager with a superior staff of people. That's because I always praised in public and criticized in private. I never thought it necessary to let others know that someone in my department didn't do his job properly. When a problem arose, I dealt one-on-one with the person involved, in private. I never raised my voice to frighten anyone into doing what was right. I discovered that people are smart enough to know who holds their pay card, so scare tactics are as unnecessary as they are unfair. I entered each of these private conversations with the assumption that both of us wanted to accomplish the same thing; perform our job with the highest degree of excellence possible. And, with a minimum of bruised feelings, correct our mistakes and get on with the job.

On the other hand, if somebody did something exceptionally well, something beyond our expectations, I made sure that as many people as possible knew about it. I always acknowledged new ideas in front of others. This encouraged others to bring ideas to me, because they knew I wouldn't plagiarize them.

Whenever possible, I praised our top performers on special occasions such as branch office meetings, sales banquets and customer conferences, as well as in our company newsletter and other publications. I never met anyone who didn't enjoy the attention. The praise must be sincere, though; otherwise you come across as a back-slapper, and lose your credibility.

Being Able to Anticipate

One of the toughest and most important traits a good leader must acquire is the ability to anticipate and develop a strategy. The generals of the world know that strategy is the craft of the warrior; they understand their own strengths and weaknesses as well as their enemies'. They then analyze these facts before they plan their attack.

No crystal ball or Ouija board will help you. First, you must put together a long-term strategic plan and a short-term operating plan that everyone agrees is realistic and attainable. Then you say, 'Look, we made our commitment. Now let's see if we can stretch beyond that.' This is known as a goal level, but the resources and commitment are set on the base plan. Second, you must prepare a definitive risk plan in case things go wrong, so you have something to fall back on. Thus you can avoid making dangerous, hip-shooting decisions, because you already thought through the problems during calm times, before they occurred.

Wayne Gretzky understands the need to anticipate. Considered perhaps the greatest hockey star in the history of the sport, he is the only professional player to score more than fifty goals in fifty or less games in a single year. He's done this for three consecutive seasons, while leading the league in scoring for the past five years. When asked his secret, he says matter-of-factly: 'I skate to where the puck is going to be, not where it has been.'

I don't think anyone is a born leader. A person who aspires to a high managerial position can develop the necessary skills if he or she is ambitious and dedicated enough. I believe that. But I know you have a head start if you like people and yourself, and adhere to a strong sense of integrity.

3

Creating a Totally Sales-Oriented Environment

. . . at IBM everybody sells! . . . Every employee has been trained to think that the customer comes first – everybody from the CEO, to the people in finance, to the receptionists, to those who work in manufacturing

Successful salespeople understand the importance of long-term customer connections. The size of their paycheck is determined to a large extent by their ability to develop sound, lasting relationships with enough customers. For the best of them, it's easy enough. They are respectful and thoughtful and go out of their way to be helpful. Most companies appreciate the need for good salespeople. Even so, what puzzles me is that so many companies have a shortsighted view of what selling is all about. They have the mistaken idea that the only salespeople in their organization are pounding the pavement, or toting a sample bag, or working the showroom. The rest of the organization is not considered as part of their marketing operation, and that's a serious mistake. Such companies may be selling a product or a service, but they aren't running a sales-oriented business. There's no way to quantify the loss in sales their tunnel vision incurs.

Doing business with a company that is not sales-oriented is usually an unpleasant experience – one we're all too familiar with. Your phone call is answered with, 'One moment please,' and before you have a chance to say hello, you're on hold. The receptionist scowls at you for interrupting a personal conversation and sends you through a maze of halls with vague directions. As you look for your destination, obviously lost, you pass a dozen employees and no one offers assistance. If this company thinks you missed a payment on its Friendly Budget Plan, you are treated as if you'd held them up with a gun; and when you prove that its accounting department screwed up, it is shrugged off without an apology. I could go on and on, but we all are familiar with people and companies who should take a course in creating a totally sales-oriented environment, emphasizing good old-fashioned courtesy.

It doesn't make any sense to invest in a sales organization or to build an advertising program designed to project a caring attitude, and then have all your good work sabotaged by someone in the credit department, or by a receptionist or secretary, or even by an unthoughtful CEO.

IBM is a sales-oriented company. That's because at IBM, *everybody sells!* That's not a slogan or a gimmick. It's a fact. Walk into the IBM building in New York or into any of its offices throughout the world and you'll get the idea. Every employee has been trained to think that the customer comes first – everybody from the CEO, to the people in finance, to the receptionists, to those who work in manufacturing.

To me, it seems utterly obvious that every employee should feel a part of the selling effort. Let's face it — everybody's salary comes out of the revenue generated by sales. When there are no sales, there is no income, and no business. It's as simple as that. Everyone in a company must understand and respect that fact, and also understand the part he or she plays in the sale.

At the same time, all employees must realize how their jobs relate to the sales force, the company's first line of attack. After all, the sales reps are the liaison people — the spokespersons who interface with the customer.

The sales-oriented shipping department understands that it can either enhance a sale or play havoc with it. As much as any service department, shipping personnel give the salespeople credibility. If because of negligence or displaced priorities an order doesn't get out of the warehouse when it was promised by the salesperson, everybody suffers. Not just the customer and the rep. Employees in the sales-oriented shipping department realize that and handle every order as if they wrote it themselves.

The sales-oriented credit department is, in a sense, an extension of the sales department. Its personnel know that if they drag their feet and delay the opening of a new account, they will cause the loss of selling time, and could even have a negative effect on their company's inventory turnover and cash flow. They think sales.

In a sales-oriented company, like IBM, all personnel who have any contact with a customer, directly or indirectly, are made to feel that they are involved with their own customer. They must also feel a responsibility toward him, never forgetting that they are being paid, in part, by that customer.

Any IBM employee you might meet, then, is trained to assume that you are a customer or a prospective customer, and should treat you as if his or her job depended on your satisfaction.

Unfortunately for the business world in general, there are too few sales-oriented, customer-driven companies. I suppose that the silver lining to that cloud is the fact that so long as this situation exists, firms that operate the way IBM does will have an edge on their competition.

Everybody Sells

IBM takes great care to project an honest-to-goodness sales-oriented environment, for customers, or anyone who visits the facilities, are expected to leave with positive feelings.

It starts with the job description of every marketing position – line or staff. Each clearly spells out the job's 'customer connection', explaining how it fits into the sales effort – how each position is part of an overall customer support system.

IBM begins imbuing its employees with its sales-oriented philosophy even before they're hired, at the very first interview. To some, the word 'imbuing' connotes brainwashing, but I don't think there's anything negative or heavy-handed in what is done. Basically, anyone who wants to work for IBM is told: 'Look, here's how we do business. At IBM, the customer comes first. We have some very specific ideas about what that means – and if you work for us we'll teach you how to treat our customers. If our attitude

64

about customers and service is incompatible with yours, we'll part ways – and the quicker the better.'

Once a person joins IBM, he or she quickly learns just how serious the company is about being a customer-oriented organization. The concept permeates the training program of every employee, regardless of position or department. Everyone learns that the bottom line is customer satisfaction, and regardless of his or her job, an employee is expected to contribute in some way to the overall marketing effort.

A firm doesn't have to be big or rich to create a sales-oriented environment. It has to be determined and sometimes hard-nosed about its attitude. Businesses that, for whatever reason, have their employees locked into rigid job descriptions must make a special point of building the sales orientation into everyone's day-to-day activities. An IBM marketing job description not only implies each employee's responsibility to the customer but also explains that it is an important factor in the employee's performance appraisal. I think it's crucial to let people know in advance that they are going to be appraised – and exactly what for. In the case of a marketing staff person, one must establish the evaluation criteria. For example, one might say: 'You are expected to spend 15 percent of your time in the field with our marketing reps'; or 'We expect you to participate in eight industry conferences'; or 'You are to keep in contact with ten customers'.

You get the idea: it's essential that everyone realizes how important the sale and the customer are, what part the employee has in the sale, and how he or she will be evaluated. It's vital that everyone be geared to respond to the customer. This certainly applies to all

IBMers. In *In Search of Excellence*, Peters and Waterman verified how the best-operated companies are customer-driven. They reported: 'The good news from excellent companies is the extent to which, and the intensity with which, the customers intrude into every nook and cranny of the business — sales, manufacturing, research, accounting.'

Money Isn't Everything

Today, most companies provide incentives for their sales force, and that's fine, especially if a substantial part of a salesperson's income is directly tied into his or her sales production. Unfortunately, most companies do not have any kind of incentive program for those who support or service the salespeople. I'm not advocating the same commission arrangement for the support staff, but I do think it's very important for everyone to think marketing, and to be rewarded for specific achievements or performances.

Of course, the most serious motivator is the job itself. Anyone who hopes to enjoy a long career with IBM must perform at a prescribed acceptable level. But if you want your people to stretch toward an excellent performance, to go beyond what's 'acceptable', or even 'very good', you should reward them with proper recognition and appreciation.

The least that can be done for an employee who does something especially nice for a customer or for a salesperson is to thank him, privately and publicly. (I almost deleted the preceding sentence because it seems so obvious, but the sad truth is that a great

many employers and managers take the genuine contributions of their staff for granted and rarely think to
express their appreciation.)

Simple awards for responsive sales- or customer-
connected ideas can promote goodwill, and point up
management's interest in sales and customers. Their
name on a plaque or their idea with proper credit in
the house organ can give people a real lift.

Tangible recognition is always welcomed and
doesn't have to be a big deal to be effective. Dinner
and a show for two is certainly a suitable way to show
appreciation. IBM calls it 'A Night on the Town'.

A weekend at a nearby resort or at a local luxury
hotel makes a nice bonus for a deserving employee.
You can be as generous as you feel is appropriate to a
particular contribution.

At IBM, some big bonuses have been given to
behind-the-scenes people to let them know how much
their customer responsiveness was appreciated. Sometimes the trappings are rather elaborate, but the
'dramas' do make a lasting impression. At a company
affair, a suitcase or a small wheelbarrow filled with a
large number of dollar bills may be dumped on a table
as the MC invites the recipient to 'Please come here
and pick up your money!' Then the MC explains what
outstanding support to the marketing function occa-
sioned this award. Any size business can give a plaque,
a television set or a check to express gratitude for
extraordinary behind-the-scenes sales support. At IBM,
it's not unusual for a secretary or a technician to be
given a small cash award or another form of recognition when the company receives a letter from a customer that commends some outstanding service
rendered. Nothing beats praise when it's deserved. No

matter what size a company is or what position an individual holds, he or she gets a real boost when a manager walks into the office and says, 'I think you did a terrific job with . . .'

While the orientation should always be to praise, you must also let people know when they're not performing satisfactorily. If you accept mediocre work, you are certain to end up with a mediocre bottom line. Criticize on a one-to-one basis, but don't be bashful about conveying your disappointment when someone lets down a customer or the field salespeople.

Every sales-oriented employee – no matter what his or her position – strengthens a company's sales and marketing efforts. It's like adding extra manpower to a work force. They become goodwill ambassadors, on and off the job, and that's important. IBM doesn't hype people to behave as though they were zealous members of some religious cult out to convert the world. But they are motivated to project a company image that radiates care for the customer, and for society in general.

Every employee is encouraged to act as if he or she were the only personal contact the customer has with the company – and to behave as if the entire company's image is dependent upon the impression that employee projects. In some cases, a behind-the-scenes person may be the only contact a customer has with the home office. In a competitive sales situation, the way a telephone inquiry is handled can be very important to the sale.

The ill will created by a lackadaisical attitude in an employee not directly involved in the selling effort can have a devastating impact on its outcome. Most businesses must realize this. It's bewildering that so few of them do anything about it.

I can't understand why any company that produces a high-quality product would allow rude, surly or apathetic employees to represent them in any phase of their operation. The installer who leaves a mess in a customer's house, the mumbler who loses patience when he's misunderstood, the clerk who acts as if he's doing a favor when he answers a question – these people make it tough on the company they work for. They should be goodwill ambassadors. They are handicaps. I'll tell you this: they wouldn't work for IBM very long.

Line Versus Staff

I must admit that when I headed IBM's US computer marketing operations – a line position – I didn't encourage corporate staff involvement. It wasn't as if corporate people weren't interested in sales; some watched the daily sales reports as avidly as a stockbroker watches the ticker tape. However, my attitude was that I had enough resources in the division to get the job done, so why complicate things. It's a fact of life that every line executive wants to run his own show without a lot of bureaucratic involvement. A bit of proprietorship seeps into your psyche, meaning: 'Keep off my turf.' The secret is not to build these barriers to where they become detrimental to getting the job done. It's important to know when to open the doors and ask for help.

After I joined the corporate staff, I felt the line divisions couldn't get along without my direction and involvement. This viewpoint may seem contradictory or even humorous, but it really isn't. It simply came about as a result of IBM's practice of moving its key people back and forth, between line and staff, so they clearly understand the responsibility of each assignment. At the same time, it emphasizes the sensitivity of a person, regardless of the job he holds, in wanting to get the day-to-day sales job done. Today, I continue to be an unabashed advocate of executive involvement in the world of sales and marketing. It's as important to have a sales-oriented corporate headquarters as it is to have a sales-oriented warehouse or credit department. It's more than just a case of vantage point.

IBM's corporate headquarters is populated with people who worked themselves up through the sales and marketing department, but it's easy to lose your sales orientation if you are separated from your sales force and your customers for any length of time. What about companies that are headed by management who never sold the products they produce, who have no sales orientation at all? How understanding and responsive can they be to their people in the field, or to their customers?

Without real understanding, a salesperson not uncommonly complains: 'If I didn't know better, I'd think the home office people were purposely trying to undermine my sales effort. It's as if they're sabotaging everything I accomplish in the field. If they won't assist me, the least they could do is stay out of my way!' When I hear sales reps talking like this, it's generally a good indication that the organization they work for has turned inward, and really doesn't understand why it's in business.

IBM's people are rotated fairly routinely between staff and line positions. It's not always convenient, but having a strong sales-minded organization is a very reasonable tradeoff. Generally, once in a staff position, employees of most companies remain in some staff slot as long as they survive the corporate wars. I think that going from line to staff is usually considered a demotion, but this is not so at IBM.

On the Firing Line

Now, it's not possible to rotate every single employee, but it is very important for your key people to have firsthand exposure to customer situations. I can't think of a better way to let the engineering, manufacturing and financial people know what goes on in the field than to *put them out in the field with a salesperson calling on customers*. It's an incredible education. You'll hear comments such as: 'It's totally different from what I had imagined.' 'I knew the sales reps were having a problem, but my interpretation was completely off base.' 'I didn't understand; no wonder my solutions were wrong.' 'I thought I had a fix on the customer's problems, but now that I've been taken through his plant, I know what we have to do at our end.'

Recently, General Motors has had factory people spend time in dealership showrooms, mingling with the customers. Not only do they see, firsthand, the customers' reactions to their product, but they also have the opportunity to hear the salespeople's 'pitch' and to listen to their complaints. The factory people go back to their plant jobs with a different perspective.

Many times I've seen IBM people develop new attitudes about customer problems after only a short time in the field. An employee handling accounts receivable gets a feel for the kind of confusion that's created when a customer is invoiced incorrectly. 'He wrote and we spoke on the phone, so I knew that he was unhappy,' a staff person said, 'but it really hit home when he looked me in the eye and said, "If the company can't bill me properly, and can't quickly expedite the correction, then how do you expect me to believe it can successfully install a computer system for us?"' In the field, you realize that the customer perceives the company as a whole, and that the foul-up of one department affects the total perception.

It's a common practice at IBM for all levels of management to meet regularly with customers. Everyone does it — department heads of accounting, education, research and development, manufacturing, and the company's top executives, as well. As corporate vice-president of marketing, I met with customers all over the world, both formally and informally.

At one lunch with a key customer, I asked about our service and if there were any problems. He answered, 'Well, Buck, overall I think your people are terrific. However . . .' He hadn't planned to complain, but we had become friendly and he felt comfortable telling me about his company's dissatisfaction with our service in one part of the country. As I probed, I discovered that one of our senior people on the account apparently had not kept up to date with certain technical aspects of the business, and the customer wasn't satisfied with this IBMer's knowledge. That afternoon I asked our regional manager to investigate discreetly. The customer's complaint was legitimate, and a serious problem was averted by getting our senior rep into a new educational program.

Sure, in my capacity as IBM's marketing vice-president I was expected to be out there mingling with customers. Well, it should be expected of *all* officers of a truly sales-oriented company. Everyone in a key managerial position should be out there constantly probing and asking the customer, 'How are we doing?' Take a leaf from New York Mayor Koch's book. He asks that question so often you might think he's patented it – but it's a good question, and if you ask it you may learn a lot from the responses you get. Then you've got to follow up quickly, or the customer will get the idea that your interest was merely rhetorical. Report back to him. Let him know what's being done. Your customer will be flattered to know how seriously you took his complaint.

The Customer on Your Turf

There are times when, instead of going to your customers, you invite them to visit you. Whether you invite one or a group, it's a great idea. At IBM, it frequently is done in a big way, with customer conferences ranging in size from fifty to a thousand participants. At these meetings, product planners, development engineers and other key technical people get an opportunity to mix and exchange ideas with these very important people. Several times a year, specific customers and a variety of industry groups – representing, say, a cross-section of the banking or the insurance field – are invited, for discussion of their industry's problems and assessment of how IBM products are meeting customers' expectations. These are important dialogues, and line and staff people are

encouraged to participate. Incidentally, it's very rein-
forcing to hear customers say positive things about the
company and not just air the problems.

Perhaps the most exciting customer sessions conducted by IBM are its Chief Executive Officers Classes.
Here are brought together in a classroom leaders from
industry, education and government. They're really
impressive groups. The representatives of industry are
either presidents or chairmen of the boards of companies that do at least a billion dollars' business a year.
The educators are presidents of leading universities,
and the politicians are usually state governors. These
five-day classes are held at the company's Poughkeepsie and San Jose facilities and are in session from eight
in the morning till eight at night. The meetings are
not a hard sell on IBM products. They focus on how
customers' operations can be improved through the
use of advanced management techniques and new
computer technologies. For ten consecutive years, I
had the privilege of being the wrap-up speaker at these
sessions. And during their chairmanships, Frank Cary
and John Opel also participated.

Now you may be thinking: 'Sure, IBM brings in
CEOs of billion-dollar companies, but how does that
apply to my business?' Naturally, I realize that smaller
firms can't duplicate these CEO classes or, for that
matter, the industry councils. However, they can do
something similar on a smaller scale. Any company
can give a luncheon or dinner, for example, to pay
tribute to its customers. Depending on your budget, a
prominent national or local guest speaker could
address the group. It's not the size that matters; it's
the environment you create when you bring your
employees and your customers together, to share ideas

and problems. It's surprising to me that so many companies don't get around to inviting any of their customers to see their operation and meet with their people, something every company should do regularly. While you might not get every customer to accept your invitation, I can promise you, at the very least, that they'll all be flattered to have been invited.

The Glue That Binds

What IBM calls account-planning sessions are conducted annually. Here, both line and customer-support people spend from three days to a week reviewing the entire status of an account. With a major customer like Citibank or General Motors, as many as fifty IBM people could be involved. In the case of a small account, the session might include a handful of IBMers.

At these meetings, the customer's business conditions are discussed, and both long-term and short-term strategies are examined. There is a review of all applications and installations of the customer's systems, its backlog, maintenance records, and so on. An action plan is set up and participants address the question: Where are we going to take this customer? What is the competitive situation? What is the right set of products? How do we give him value? These questions are discussed with the customer and his participation is a vital part of the development of the plan. A wonderful partnership arrangement evolves. The customer has a well-documented action plan that covers the upcoming year as well as years to come.

One of the best things about the account-planning

sessions is the productive working relationship that develops between the customer and IBMers. It's not simply a matter of marketing reps and system engineers working closely with the customer. Many others can be involved – planning people, engineers, service people, administrative employees, and others – all working closely with the customer. While many good things result from these sessions, one obvious benefit is a very enlightened support system to back up the marketing rep.

The IBM account-planning session should give a business of any size some constructive ideas. In the majority of cases, these meetings are conducted on a much smaller scale than what I have just described, but the same basic principle is applied. Time is allocated to reflect upon IBM's relationship with each customer, and to put together a brief history that facilitates an action plan. A small company can do the same thing. It might take only a single afternoon session at your office, or at the customer's place of business. The important thing is to get all your people, particularly the behind-the-scenes ones, involved in working with the customer and developing a partnership relationship.

The Top 100

I could visit an IBM branch anywhere in the United States, Canada, South America, the Far East, Europe and Asia and ask: 'What can you tell me about your top accounts?' I would then be shown an extensive up-to-date file on every one of them. There'd be a booklet containing data ranging from current systems installed to the education programs in effect. These documents are kept current to make sure the needs of each of these customers are understood, and if there's a change in the sales force, new people can be informed quickly on the status of the account.

The short-term and long-term plans for major customers were always available not only to me but to all senior management, including the president and the chairman of the board.

Every business should keep similar data on its top accounts, but by no means is 100 a magic number. Just how many and how you arrange them depends on a number of variables. Sales volume and sales potential are basic orientations, or maybe you will focus on what I call 'leadership' accounts, those that are the most prestigious and make the greatest impact on their industry. And while you are committed to giving outstanding service to all your customers, certain ones are what I refer to as your company's family jewels. You've worked very hard to obtain them, and you want to stay on top of things so you *never lose them*.

These account profiles and action plans are an important tool and should be available for review at the drop of a hat. You should not have to go digging for information when a problem develops with a top account. Although I know of many companies whose executives don't even know who their top customers are, such a situation at IBM is inconceivable to me.

Executive Involvement

A company cannot afford to excuse its high-ranking executives from participating in its sales effort. IBM believes that. The executive who gets his 'feel' for the marketplace from reports, trade publications and an occasional meeting with a customer is going to have a shallow understanding of the problems in the field. Consequently, top IBM executives not only spend some of their time traveling with reps, but also have key customers assigned to them. These executives – who are responsible for working with perhaps three or four customers – are from all parts of the company: marketing, manufacturing, development labs, etc. They stay in touch with their accounts in person and by phone. They ask for suggestions, make recommendations, present updated information about technology and express thanks for the business. Sometimes they invite a customer to spend a day at a plant, laboratory or headquarters; at other times, they take a few key IBMers out to visit the customer. The objective of this program is to develop a sales-oriented executive group – the most sensitive possible. It avoids management's living in an isolated cocoon, out of touch with reality.

This work with customers is always done with the co-operation and help of the local IBM marketing rep. Thus, besides a firsthand view of some of the day-to-day problems of the customer, the executive gets a real education about selling in the field. Other benefits gained include a possible short-circuiting, by customer and rep, of company bureaucracy. Over the years, some companies I worked with included United Airlines, Bank of America, Dow Chemical, Carter Hawley Hale,

Standard Oil of California, and Boeing Corporation. The people in these companies felt comfortable contacting me directly as well as working through the IBM branch office, and I particularly enjoyed being on an informal, first-name basis with all levels of their management. For some executives in other areas of the business, these assignments are especially exciting and enlightening because they afford a rare firsthand knowledge of the marketplace.

The Company Heroes

The real heroes in every truly market-driven company are the sales reps. It is they who find out what the customers want and need, and that's where it all begins. Thanks to the marketing reps, IBM's engineering and manufacturing departments build what the customer needs. Our reps are never told, 'Here's a product that we've created – now you go out and create a need for it.' All employees know that salespeople are the catalysts who generate the company's business.

It bewilders me that some companies consider their sales force to be a necessary evil, something they wish they could eliminate – an expense they are forever whittling away at. These companies have little or no respect for their salespeople and more often than not treat them as though they were adversaries. They cut territories unnecessarily, raise quotas unrealistically, reduce commission rates whenever they can, and try to bully their salespeople into performing. The company usually gets what it deserves – a sales force that's angry, unhappy, unresponsive and nonproductive.

Companies like this give the sales force only minimal headquarters support, and cry out in pain when everything they try falls short of their expectations.

These are not sales-oriented companies. Staff doesn't communicate with line – the left hand doesn't know what the right hand is doing. Salespeople are generally left stranded in their territories without selling tools and information. And the customer is a victim of such companies' foolishness and inefficiency. In time, these companies self-destruct. Sadly, they are poisoning themselves, and they won't know it until it's too late. They have only to realize that it doesn't take a great deal of money or brains to build a successful sales-oriented company. A little money, a few brains and a lot of caring will do it.

I wear my admiration for creative salespeople like a badge for all to see. Every company, starting with its highest management, should make it known to every one of its employees that the salesperson is a VIP. That is how he or she is treated at IBM. It's not unusual for a small group of the top salespeople to be invited to the home office for informal meetings, a private lunch or dinner meeting with top management, and a friendly chat with the chairman of the board. In addition to being great morale-builders for the salesperson, these meetings have a tremendous impact on the total organization. If the chairman and other top executives think enough of sales reps to have these small get-togethers, it makes a strong statement about how selling is valued by the company! It's such a natural thing for IBM to do, but other companies simply don't think in these terms. I know of a salesperson who was the leading producer not only in his company but in his entire industry, and yet he had never met the company's president or chairman. Even when he let it be known that he'd like to meet them, his request was denied. I can't understand the mentality of that company's management! They had a golden opportunity to give well-deserved recognition that would have had a ripple effect on the entire organization. No wonder salespeople too often accuse management of not coming down from their ivory tower!

Praise and recognition are fundamental at IBM, but I must admit that an extra effort is devoted to recognizing exceptional performance in the marketing arena. Some salespeople reach star or celebrity status not only in the company but in the industry – and they deserve it. Let's face it – the salesperson is the *source* in business.

Finally – and it should go without saying – a company must be generous in compensating its sales reps. Underpaying them clearly tells everyone you think they're not important. If they *are* valuable to your business, they deserve to be compensated accordingly. You have to put your money where your mouth is. It's important for IBM to maintain a leadership role through its compensation plan. To ensure this, the total compensation package is routinely evaluated against other information-processing companies, as well as businesses outside the industry. IBM simply wants to make sure that its sales force receives a premium for outstanding performance. This practice helps attract, and retain, top performers.

Creating More Selling Time

In a truly sales-oriented environment, everyone is working in harmony to make the sales rep's time more productive. Everyone is asking questions like: 'How can I get the order processed sooner?' 'How can I guarantee quick delivery?' 'How can I improve my job to support the customer?' 'How can I enhance the quality of the product?' When everyone in the company is thinking along these lines, the sales rep is going to get the kind of support that is needed to serve the customer.

I don't like it when a salesperson who works all day in the field is burdened with hours of paperwork in the evening. Good reps save their paperwork for nonselling time, and those extra long hours are bound to take their toll in energy, if not in enthusiasm. IBM gives constant attention to reducing unnecessary detail work by the sales rep, and wherever possible tries to mechanize his paperwork. For example, every IBM salesperson has available a terminal that can be used to look up a customer's account in a matter of seconds and access everything needed to provide fine service.

Shortly after I was named president of IBM's Data Processing Division in 1967, I initiated a program for the thousands of employees who worked with me. I wanted everyone to be more responsive to the customer, and a campaign was set up requesting suggestions for improvements on our ways of doing things. New in my position, I asked everyone to give me advice on running the division. Each employee was invited to finish the statement: 'If I were president of the Data Processing Division . . .' I announced that I would respond to every suggestion, and recognition, from dinners to money awards, would be given for the best ideas. The program was a huge success, generating several thousand suggestions from marketing reps, service personnel, systems engineers, programmers, secretaries, branch officers and headquarters people. The most striking thing about the responses was that people were concerned not only with current operations but also with the future. Proposals covered every conceivable subject related to the success of the division, including customer relations, asset management, recruitment, personnel development, education, policy and marketing programs. These ideas were considered by the division, and were also forwarded to IBM's Suggestion Plan, where they became eligible for corporate awards. I think it worked so well because people took it seriously – and knew that they would be taken seriously.

One thing I learned from listening to the people in the field is that the bureaucracy of a corporation can really handicap a sales organization that's designed to react swiftly to the needs of its customers. Rules, regulations and procedures are never intended to stifle, but unless there's a conscious effort to keep them in check, they can be suffocating. What developed at IBM is a pretty good example of what can happen.

Over the years, an extensive library of procedures and directives, called branch office manuals, was built. In every branch office, bookcases were packed with thousands of pages of 'how to' and 'what for' material. Volumes instructed, in minute detail, how to process an order, how to submit reports, how to requisition supplies, when to raise the flag, etc., etc. This stuff was taken very seriously by management people. Each new page that was added to this ever-growing body of knowledge was one more headache for the rep in the field. I must admit that as president of the division, I could avoid most of the irritating procedures that filled the manuals. (The fact that people in high positions are usually immune to this type of paperwork, some of which they author, contributes to the problem.)

Well, the complaints from the field got to me and I decided to do something. Accompanied by several headquarters executives, I flew to Salt Lake City unannounced and physically removed the complete set of IBM branch office manuals.

The first reaction was: 'How can we operate without them? How will we know what to do? It will be chaos!'

'Use common sense,' I replied. 'Do what's right for the customer, and above all, make it easier for the IBM people to do business. Rewrite the book so we can be more responsive, lighter on our feet.' Then I flew to Saint Louis and went through the same thing at our branch there.

Within ninety days we had a new set of guidelines, which became the standard operating procedure for the entire division. The revised manual was a quarter of the original. More important, hours of unnecessary paperwork had been eliminated.

The ease of modern communication is usually considered a blessing, but sometimes it can be abused. When a few of our branch managers complained about the amount of paper that was crossing their desks, I wanted to get a feel for what they were up against, and asked the mailroom to send me every piece of paper the branches were receiving. In a week, my desk was covered with so much material that there was no room for anything else. Obviously, the complaints from the field were justified.

Our branch offices were being deluged with paper from all over the division: from product managers complaining that their product was not selling in some area, and wanting the branch manager to initiate a new program for them; from education centers asking for help in filling a class; from financial managers wanting to borrow a few people for a week to participate in a task force. Along with requests that had branch managers juggling their staff at the same time they were trying to meet their own objectives, there was an inundation of promotional material, product information, directives, price changes, procedural modifications. You name it, they got it. To relieve the situation and free our people for selling, installing and servicing, I ordered a control point where information was prioritized. Not only was the flow of unnecessary paper curtailed; the number of people who could communicate directly with the branch offices was reduced.

Bureaucracy, with the paper it generates, can take on a life of its own. It can exist for its own sake, insensitive to the mission and goals of a company. For me, there must be a continuous effort to improve the ability to serve the customer, by creating more selling time for the sales reps and the branch managers.

4

Building a Superior Marketing Organization

. . . top management should spend 40 to 50 percent of its time educating and motivating its people . . .

Thomas Watson, Sr, believed that IBM's annual investment in education, training and internal communication should increase at a rate that is greater than the company's rate of growth. He wanted the people who worked for him to understand the goals of the company, and to know that each person's contribution was important toward achieving those goals.

Watson, who had been employed by National Cash Register, first as a marketing rep and then as a sales manager, recognized the striking parallel between a salesperson's success and the amount of home office support he received. He knew that a salesperson needed not only proper sales training and product knowledge but also inspiration, and a dynamic organization ready with backup support. Watson's successor, Tom, Jr, began his IBM career in sales and, like his father, understood the importance of the marketing rep. Since its earliest days, then, 'Everybody thinks selling' has been a dominant theme at IBM.

Like the Watsons and thousands of other IBMers who have had management positions, I began my career with the company as a marketing rep. In this chapter, I will discuss IBM's marketing operation. Much of what has made that company great can be emulated by any sales organization.

The Talent Search

IBM recruits top people.

Although I don't believe in a 'naturally born' salesperson, I do think some candidates have greater potential than others. IBM doesn't hire people at random. Its recruitment program is truly a selective talent search.

IBM recruits from approximately 350 colleges across the country, focusing on 100 top schools. Selected executives act as liaisons to thirty-two key schools, including Harvard, Illinois, Penn State, Purdue, the University of Texas and UCLA. Grades, student activities, athletics, leadership roles and communication skills are important considerations. About half of the recruits have technical degrees in hard sciences, such as math, engineering and physics; about 40 percent have business degrees, and the rest are art and science majors. Approximately 40 percent are women.

In 1984, the average student recruit had a 3.65 grade point average. But this did not rule out the C student who made an outstanding impression during his personal interview – the most important factor of the selection process.

To the surprise of many placement officers, only firstline managers do the actual hiring for IBM. After all, if you hold these managers accountable and sible for the company's objectives, then you gi the freedom to pick and choose the people th

IBM has a corporate recruiting organization that sets guidelines, teaches techniques, maintains liaison with the various college placement offices and coordinates recruiting activities among the various divisions. Because of its size, IBM needs this superstructure. In 1984 alone, the company had more than 1,300,000 job applications!

While most marketing people are recruited on college campuses, others apply on their own, or respond to IBM advertisements for individuals with specific skills. One important source of talent is referrals. Unlike many companies, IBM encourages its employees to recommend friends and relatives, considering it a wonderful endorsement. I could never agree with company policies that prohibit hiring immediate family of employees. However, all hiring and all promotion are based on individual merit and nobody receives special preference. There are regular complaints by IBMers whose children are not hired. It's a source of great personal pride that my three children all joined IBM in marketing and are enjoying successful careers with the company.

Since IBM operates with a well-defined value system, it's essential that the young people recruited into the company are comfortable and compatible with those values. Important as it is for the interviewer to do an honest job of describing the company and its opportunities, it's even more important for the interviewee to speak his mind and present his wares. He must be given the time to sell himself.

An applicant is expected to know something about IBM and have an idea of why and how he might fit in. After all, he is applying for a position in marketing!

I like an applicant who is assertive and asks questions about the company's philosophy, its pay range, how people are promoted, the training program. The questions show thoughtfulness and intelligence. An applicant shouldn't attempt to overwhelm the interviewer with his or her personality. I advise young people to ask questions that show their interest in establishing a long-term partnership with the company.

I don't believe in just taking from the campus. A person successful in business has what I've called a 'civic rent' to pay. There are many creative programs at schools across the country where business people can become involved. I myself have participated in the Executive in the Classroom programs at Purdue and Tennessee, Penn State's Distinguished Speaker program, and the Colgate Darden School program at the University of Virginia. Though my purpose in being on campus wasn't to recruit, I met many outstanding students, some of whom subsequently joined IBM.

Every executive should visit at least one or two college campuses every year. The campus is a good place not only to find out what young people in this country think but also to become energized. You should let students know that ethics, rewards and excitement exist in the world of American business. It's vital for students to get a mixture of the theory being taught in the classroom and the practicality of the business world. This type of participation builds a better bridge of understanding between classroom and boardroom. Although business people are welcomed on college campuses today, there were periods when we were not so well received. At such times, a special effort must be made to hear the students' message and make sure they hear yours.

Theory and Practice

IBM would never send an untrained or a partially trained person into the field. What representatives say and do, and how they say and do it, is too important to the company's image and credibility. And it could shorten the career of a potentially good salesperson to go into the field unprepared.

IBM's training program is well funded, planned and structured, so by the time the trainee is finished, he has the skills to meet the customer with confidence. A weak training program almost guarantees high turnover — and that always costs more than an effective training program. Turnover can shatter a sales organization's morale and frustrate the customer who is dependent on the rep for service and advice. In recent years, IBM lost less than 3 percent of its first-year marketing reps, so from the company's point of view, the recruiting and training programs work.

IBM sales and systems engineer trainees receive twelve months of initial training — field experience combined with formal classroom work. About 75 percent of the training is at the branch office location and 25 percent at one of IBM's national education centers. A branch office training manager will oversee the IBM trainee's education program, which includes self-paced modules on everything from the company's culture, values and beliefs to basic knowledge of the full product line. Trainees spend time with marketing people on customer calls to get a feel for the business.

In addition, it is not uncommon for the new kid on the block to make his first formal product demonstration to the most critical audience – the veteran reps – at a branch office meeting. Sometimes the constructive criticism can be devastating, but the trainee gains confidence and earns the respect of his peers. The branch office takes great care in ensuring that its trainees are ready for each phase of marketing training. Just as IBM would never send an unqualified rep to meet with a customer, it would never send an unqualified trainee to one of the schools. It simply doesn't make good business sense.

The first marketing school covers some of the more formal aspects of the way IBM does business, including sales policies and marketing practices, in addition to computer concepts and IBM products. Learning to sell begins on the second day of class. (Many organizations barely discuss the art of selling in their training sessions, dealing with it almost as an afterthought.) In the classroom, IBM trainees learn about the company's support structure and how to use it. They study the competition and begin to develop general business skills.

This process of theory and practice continues as the IBM trainee moves closer to becoming a qualified sales rep or systems engineer. The trainee sees the practical side of the classroom work when he or she returns to the branch. The fieldwork is followed by another four weeks of classroom sessions, referred to as 'heartbreak hill': intense schooling from 8 A.M. to 6 P.M., and homework that keeps the trainee working past midnight. The courses were designed so that no one could finish them, and for a reason. In the world of business, people must learn how to manage their time. They must determine 'What is enough effort?' 'Is it better to stay up all night rather than study until ten?' In the beginning of the program, the trainees are graded as if they were in college – that is, tests are objective, and the results are based on how much information is retained. As they progress in the program, the testing becomes more subjective. Trainees perform sales demonstrations, and although they might have their facts down pat, they might get a poor grade because of a weak presentation. The facts must be presented in simple terms that spell value and benefits. A customer won't judge a salesperson on what he knows, but on how well he communicates what he knows. The business world is subjective, so that's what sales trainees must be prepared to deal with.

Occasionally trainees think and act as if they are still in college, and object to a specific phase of the training program. 'We don't think it's fair that the instructors have all the power and decide the curriculum. We think we should have more say about it.' Student power!

When this happens, they're told: 'You probably paid fifteen thousand dollars a year to go to school. Now we're paying you. So we decide what's best. This is the economic imperative and one of the first things for you to learn about business.' It's a welcome-to-the-real-world lesson, and the demands for student power have always been short-lived.

Generally, the trainees thrive on IBM's rigorous training program, the long hours and the stiff competition. It really is tough on them – fourteen to fifteen hours of intense study each day – but seldom does anyone complain, and rarely does anyone drop out.

The top people IBM recruits are highly motivated,

and in the formal training program these individuals want to perform to the best of their abilities. One reason the trainees take the education program so seriously is that students are evaluated each step of the way. At the conclusion of marketing training, an Excellence in Marketing award is presented and a class president designated.

Who Make the Best Teachers?

Many companies assign the job of training new people to their least productive sales reps. Unwilling to give up the revenue of top producers, they think they are saving money. I believe that the sales force is far too important to be trained by mediocre people. The best teachers are a company's top sales staff, for not only do they understand selling techniques; they have the keenest perceptions, and marketing acumen that is second to none. It's important, too, that your instructors be heroes and role models. Proud of their accomplishments in the field, they should be able to project that pride in the classroom. It probably *will* cost some sales to pull the top producers out of the field, but a well-trained sales force will pay back the short-term losses in spades.

Not every top salesperson is able to teach, so IBM has been very careful in selecting its instructors. Marketing instructors go through rigorous training before they are permitted to lead a class. An IBM instructor teaches for no more than eighteen to twenty-four months, so there is an influx of fresh experiences, brought in by up-to-date salespeople. The assignment has proved to be a stepping-stone for the marketing people, as 75 percent of instructors are promoted to first-line manager positions.

IBM's instructor-trainee ratio is one to ten. In addition, top marketing and systems engineering reps are invited to be guest instructors for each class. Trainees hear straight from the source how a significant order was won – or lost – just a few days before, and benefit from an even closer instructor-trainee ratio. At the same time, the guest instructor is, in a sense, auditioning for a new assignment.

Team Selling

Unlike students in most classrooms, IBM trainees are taught to work as a team. For sixteen years of schooling, students are told, 'Don't look at anyone's paper. Do your own work.' Now, for the first time, IBM trainees are told, 'Here's the problem. The four of you must solve it together.' Initially, most trainees don't know how to react to this different approach to problem solving. They have to learn to share and cooperate intellectually, as they work on a single assignment that requires each of them to fulfill specific tasks. The problem cannot be solved unless they work together. This closely approximates the type of team effort and cooperation that the rep will be expected to display in the field. In our industry, sales reps are constantly working with and relying upon the skills of others – specialists in accounting and manufacturing, inventory control and engineering. Since reps assigned to large national accounts always work in teams, it is essential for trainees to become productive team members as soon as possible. At the same time, the entrepreneurial spirit must be maintained.

The Structured Sales Call

Teaching the structured sales call is a fundamental part of IBM marketing training. Not a single day goes by during the entire first year without it being part of the trainee's education program. I am not implying that a 'canned' sales presentation is used; it's not possible in our business. However, IBMers learn certain basic messages and techniques, which are incorporated into every presentation.

The objectives of the demonstration or presentation are always stated. This includes why you are there and what you hope to accomplish. The features, functions and benefits of the product are clearly articulated and demonstrated. Trainees learn questioning techniques and listening skills, how to manage objections and ask for the order. If the customer says the product costs too much, you must first find out if this is a valid objection. A cost-justification proposal won't get the order if other factors underlie the objection.

IBM is constantly refining and honing the sales methodology that is taught in every sales school. There's continual role-playing in the classes, with the instructor as customer, whose problems the trainees demonstrate their ability to solve. These sessions are closely monitored and the trainees are critiqued on both strengths and weaknesses. A student is assessed and measured in several key areas, including communication skills, presentation/demonstration techniques, customer interaction and general business knowledge. For every sales call and product demonstration a student gives, he receives personal feedback from his instructor.

IBM conducts one of the most ambitious and sophisticated techniques ever developed for sales training – the Armstrong Case Study, focusing on a fictitious international conglomerate with hotel chains, marinas, retail outlets, and manufacturing and sporting goods divisions. There are detailed profiles of engineers, financial executives, marketing people, the chief operating officer and the chief executive officer. The profiles incorporate personality characteristics, attitudes and even past decisions.

IBM created an incredibly lifelike environment, with instructors enacting Armstrong personnel. The trainees are required to make a series of complicated calls on various people within the organization. Facing dozens of problems and challenges, they must deal with almost everyone in the Armstrong organization, from receptionists to the board of directors. The study is so realistic and the 'actors' so convincing that every participant treats the case study as seriously as IBM intended. The exercise culminates in a simulated customer meeting which includes presentation of the study findings, the IBM solution and getting the order.

Customers in the Classroom

Not only does IBM bring its top sales and technical people into the training centers; it invites customers as well. Their participation creates a real-world atmosphere because they discuss specific problems affecting their businesses. The trainee learns that salespeople can cost the customer money in terms of valuable time, and that a business person is selective about whom he will see. The customer will quickly terminate a sales presentation that doesn't immediately interest or benefit him. Hearing this from someone he or she may someday call on makes a strong impression on the trainee. Customers are usually flattered to participate in education, so don't be shy about seeking their cooperation and counsel.

The Profound Difference

During the three years that I was president of the Data Processing Division, I made it my business to meet with every individual who completed our rigorous sales training program. When I became vice-president of marketing, I continued this practice as often as I could.

This meant addressing twenty to twenty-five final sales training classes and delivering what might be called the graduation speech. Each year, I was able to meet, face to face, with five hundred to a thousand IBMers who were about to go into their first sales territory assignment.

I got a pretty good fix on the quality of our recruiting

efforts and the effectiveness of our training program. In addition, I was able to provide tactical and strategic direction, and at the same time challenge the group to meet their objectives.

From the students' perspective, they met firsthand with the president of the division. A trainee in a corporation of thousands of people can feel a million miles away from the company's management. Obviously I didn't want that. Besides, I wanted them to know that their top management understood the marketplace and was willing to listen to any problems or new ideas they might have.

Recently, I addressed a class of IBM marketing trainees in New York City at the wrap-up session of their training program. In the new IBM Madison Avenue building, surrounded by these highly trained reps, I could feel their camaraderie and high spirits. This was the gist of my message to them:

> You know that you have participated in a superior training program, and that you will represent a product line that's the envy of the industry. You feel secure with the knowledge that you have both technical and application support systems to help you provide value to the customer. All of this gives you a sense of great strength. And it should, because you know that you have the means to get the job done. Of course, the real test comes when you walk out the door and are on your own. At times you will call on prospects and even some customers who won't be impressed by the name and reputation of IBM, or care how much we invest in research and development. They have a multitude of problems that need solutions. They

want answers, information, new ideas. In order to help them, you must draw upon your personal strength and all that you have learned during your training. This is the challenge you face. And part of the beauty and excitement of selling comes with the knowledge that you – one person – can make a profound difference.

The Disciplined Sales Rep

When a customer is receptive, a sales career seems like a piece of cake. It doesn't require discipline to make calls when everything is going well. That's easy.

However, if he makes enough calls, a rep will have doors slammed in his face sooner or later. It's something that comes with every territory. Rejection hurts the best of us, but when a sales rep gets shot down several times in a row, it takes discipline to keep going, especially when there's nobody following him to make sure he keeps plugging away. The best and most effective discipline is self-imposed.

In the 1950s, like all IBM marketing reps I was required to submit, weekly, an hour-by-hour, day-by-day plan of how I would spend my time in the field. This was not only burdensome; it was a nightmare to administer. The company eliminated these reports in the 1960s, thinking that with the right people, it wasn't necessary to dictate how hard they must work to achieve success. IBM no longer uses formalized call activity forms. In effect, IBM said to the people in the field: 'We have enough respect for you to believe that you're going to give us a fair day's work for a fair day's pay.' However, the marketing rep's day-to-day work habits eventually surface when a documented account plan for each customer is reviewed.

Although the individual doesn't report his daily activities, IBM develops accurate records by a quarterly survey of the entire sales force. Every marketing organization needs to have a formalized method for getting information from its sales force – it must know how its people are spending their time in the field. IBM's Field Reporting System provides the company with information on how much time is being spent selling and servicing a specific product. From this reporting system it also gets the expense-to-revenue ratios by product, which help in setting the right price and determining the real profit being generated per product. IBM also finds out if the support structure is functioning as it should for all product categories. Perhaps more manpower is required to support a particular product. With effective reporting, the company may discover that more education and training than had been originally planned is needed to sell some of its products. As you can see, the field report is more than simply a device to measure an individual's sales activity.

First Impressions

When people hear the name IBM, I'm sure many different images come to mind, especially for those who don't really know the company. A while back, I heard it said that IBM stood for 'I've Been Moved'. People thought of IBM as an impersonal monolithic organization that disregarded the rights and feelings of its employees; a company with no wild ducks, its representatives all cloned to fly in formation. Over the years, many myths developed, and that can't be controlled. But when the opportunity arises (like now), I am delighted to project an IBM image that is rooted in reality.

One of the first questions asked by the curious is not about IBM's size or its products or its history, but rather: 'Is it true that IBM requires you to wear a dark conservative suit, winter or summer, a white shirt and a quiet tie?' That's the number one question! Now, IBM has no written policy that tells a person how to dress: that's a fact. But to be completely truthful, there is an unwritten dress code that's as effective as if it were engraved in steel – or as if it had a loaded gun behind it. So the honest answer to the question is 'Yes,' or at least, 'Sort of.' The first reaction to this is often feigned surprise: 'In the mid-eighties? You gotta be kidding!'

Well, let's talk about uniforms for a minute. In all kinds of businesses, people work in uniforms and no one thinks anything about it. The uniform is usually designed to help the wearer perform his job as efficiently as possible. A surgeon does his work in a gown, a dentist in a white coat, a policeman in blue; an athlete wears an outfit that will give him the most freedom and the best protection, and make him easily identifiable to any spectators who may be present. Musicians in a symphony orchestra wear formal dress, and I imagine that if you attended a concert and found each of them dressed in informal attire of their choice, you'd be disconcerted. And have you ever played tennis or golf with a person who was 'out of uniform'? Weren't you distracted?

That's one of the points of IBM's unwritten dress

code. Clothes should not be such as to distract people. Men and women who are on the job representing IBM wear business suits. That's because IBM is serious about its business and wants that attitude projected to its customers by its front people. Besides, what's wrong with dressing for the occasion? Or being expected to? I don't wear a business suit when I'm at a sports event or a casual dinner or a neighborhood movie. And if I wore a suit at a backyard barbecue, would the proponents of 'wear whatever turns you on' applaud me for my individuality? I doubt it.

Some of the critics of the business suit complain that it's an uncomfortable way to dress. That makes no sense to me at all. What makes a loud plaid sports jacket more comfortable than a blue suit jacket? The colors? Certainly not the material or the cut. If your suit fits you, it will be comfortable. And the only time that I felt uncomfortable in a white shirt was when I tried to squeeze my 16 neck into a 15½ collar.

One of the most frequent complaints IBM hears is this: 'When you impose a dress code you're inhibiting self-expression, individuality and creativity.' My response is usually: 'Baloney!' No company has put more time and money into developing the creative talents of its staff than IBM; and none of its research or observations leads IBM to believe that the way its employees dress is in any way a negative. In fact, the conviction is that IBM people's mode of dress is a real plus for them and the company. I'll explain.

Everyone who calls on a customer or prospect for IBM wears a suit – that includes service people, those who call on an account to repair a typewriter or a computer. I know that most people expect a repairman to show up in a pair of coveralls, or some other form of work clothes. Tom Watson, Sr, had observed service people with other companies who were not treated with the same respect as salespeople who dressed in business suits. That didn't seem right to Watson. He wanted those talented technicians to be respected and he wanted them to have self-esteem. For this reason, all IBM repair people and installers have always dressed the same way as the marketing reps. It's greatly influenced their reception in the field, and I'm sure it makes them feel better about themselves.

About a half century after Tom Watson decided that the way you dressed affected the way you were perceived, and the way you were perceived affected the way you were treated, John T. Molloy wrote *Dress for Success*. Watson's beliefs were supported, time after time, by the studies done for this best-selling book. Receptionists who ignored the fellow in the sport jacket were warm and friendly to the one dressed in a pin-striped suit. Executive secretaries who wouldn't set up an appointment for a person with a stylish but flamboyant hairdo set one up without a hitch for the person with a fresh conservative haircut. It goes on and on.

Incidentally, almost all the criticism of IBM's 'dress code' comes from outside the company. Neither employees nor customers complain. Enough said about clothes.

Now, for the record, it's true that in the past IBM did move a lot of people around. It was partly the times. After World War II, it seemed that half the households in the nation were on wheels, traveling between cities on cavernous moving vans. IBM contributed its share to the traffic jams. The relocations almost always involved a promotion and an improved opportunity for the employee; not good was management's dim view of anyone who turned down an opportunity when it was offered. The future of the employee was not nearly as bright as it would have been had he complied.

Sometimes it takes a while, but attitudes change. Society began looking with a critical eye at the whole idea of families being uprooted. And so did IBM. It became a moral issue. Was it right to relocate an employee, and of course his or her family, strictly for the company's convenience? IBM wisely and happily responded to the changing times by revising its relocation policies. In addition to the personal problems relocation caused, it was very expensive to the company and often disruptive to the customer. Today, no IBMer can be transferred at the whim of his manager. At least three other candidates must be considered for a position. Nor can anyone be moved within two years of the date of a previous relocation without having both his immediate manager and the division president approve it. When a manager carries the decision up the line, people are less likely to be moved indiscriminately. Of course, IBMers may still be relocated, but not as often and never out of fear of losing their jobs or crippling their careers.

It's been years since IBM changed its policy, and I don't hear the 'I've Been Moved' jokes very often anymore; but it took a long time to shake it. There's something to be learned from that – you're stuck with the image you project, and you're perceived that way for a long time, so you have to give a good deal of thought to what you do and how you do it.

Stay-in-Touch Management

When I moved into management, I was determined not to be viewed as one of those executives who, following a promotion, divorced himself from the selling end of the business. I knew I would be most effective in marketing if I had firsthand knowledge about what was happening in the field. I made up my mind that I would never be too busy to visit our customers, in the company of the marketing rep responsible for each account. I would thank them for their business, talk about IBM's strategies and listen to their views of our products and services. And it was exhilarating for me. Besides, it gave me the opportunity to show off a little, to demonstrate that the person at the top was as knowledgeable as were the people on the firing line. Marketing reps want action-oriented management. A sales force loses confidence in managers who isolate themselves in ivory towers. And so do the customers.

As president of IBM's computer division in the US and later as vice-president of marketing, I spent at least 25 percent of my time meeting with customers, either in the field or at industry meetings. Each year I committed myself to a specific number of customer calls.

Communicating with the Sales Force

IBM has one of the largest sales forces in the world. And because it's spread out all over the globe, the problems of communicating with this army of marketing reps, systems engineers and administrative people are especially complicated. But the sales force has a compelling need for information, and it's the responsibility of management to get that information to them.

Just how management goes about it is determined by the nature of the information and its degree of urgency. Information of general interest may appear in *Think*, an IBM in-house bimonthly publication that's distributed to more than 200,000 US employees and thousands more overseas. Each division and facility has its own in-house publication. Bulletin boards at every IBM location contain news of a more immediate nature.

Some important messages are first given to a group of high-ranking executives, who relay them to the rest of the organization. Early each January, for example, IBM's CEO delivers to the company's assembled top officers the plans and goals for the next twelve months and for years ahead. I vividly recall John Opel's calling out at one such meeting the four goals set by IBM for the 1980s to ensure its continued leadership: One, to grow with the industry, not only in traditional areas such as mainline computers but also in newer areas. Two, to exhibit leadership both in the development and production of high-quality, reliable products and in sales and service. Three, to be *the* most efficient and effective in everything it does – *the* low-cost producer, *the* low-cost seller, *the* low-cost servicer and *the* low-cost administrator. And four, to sustain profitability, which funds the growth of the business.

The January meeting lasts only one day, but as many as 250 people attend from all over the world. Following that, each executive who attended passes down the company's goals through his chain of command. Every branch manager around the world holds a special kick-off meeting that highlights the corporate goals and specifically addresses the divisional and local targets. These are, in essence, sales rallies to motivate the field force.

One year, when we were excited about a significant change, I thought its importance would be dramatized if the sales force got the information directly from me. Our communications people videotaped my message and copies were forwarded immediately to all branches. A day or two later, my speech was delivered to thousands of reps throughout the entire marketing organization. On other occasions, IBM rented movie theatres in large metropolitan areas to make important announcements via closed-circuit television.

In 1981, when IBM's marketing was completely reorganized, there was concern about the magnitude of the change and its effect on the individual IBMer. A vast sophisticated educational program was launched, which utilized slides, videotapes, written question-and-answer handouts, as well as a personal presentation by an IBM executive. The message was delivered simultaneously throughout the country.

Nothing is more frustrating for a rep than to have a customer give him a bit of information about his company that he didn't already know. Sometimes the 'news' slips out prematurely and quickly feeds the rumor mill. More often than not, it's misinformation, which needs to be quickly dispelled. This kind of problem is handled by getting on the phones right away or by sending the correct information to the branches via our telecommunication system.

When I assumed the management of IBM's Western Region, I wanted to let everyone in each of my sixty branch offices know what kind of guy they were going to have to deal with. I decided that the best way wasn't necessarily the quickest – or the easiest. I would visit all sixty branches and meet everyone in person. It took two weeks and lots of hours in the air – covering every major city in the western United States, from L.A. to Dallas to Seattle to San Diego. I traveled with the heads of Personnel and Service, and almost every day we had breakfast, lunch and dinner in a different city, meeting with IBMers, making speeches and conducting private conferences. It was a very tiring trip, and we joked about the number of times my companions had to listen to me speak. I'd coax them, 'Please keep from falling asleep while I'm delivering my speech.'

At the end of the tour, the three of us were exhausted, excited and fulfilled.

Then, in 1965, we experienced some difficult times as a result of a slump in the aerospace industry, a major source of the Western Region's business. Numerous changes had to be made, which many times meant physically moving people to other areas of opportunity. In order to get our people to extend themselves so that we could meet our goals for the year, I ran a motivational program which had the theme 'The Winning of the West'. Wall-sized posters were sent to all the branch offices, and weekly meetings with twenty-five IBMers at a time were conducted at my office in Los Angeles. It took six months, but I met with every marketing rep in the region – hundreds of them. I would explain our strategy in great detail and ask each rep for a personal commitment. A lot of hoopla and fun were incorporated into these gatherings. As we began to turn things around, special awards of appreciation were given for productivity and valuable feedback from the field.

It's vitally important for all levels of management to have some form of one-to-one communication with its sales force. It's a matter of finding out, firsthand, what's going on, and it does wonders for the salespeople's morale. You must let them know you care; if you can't do that, you can't manage them effectively. Every field manager stays in close phone contact with people in remote locations who are not seen daily or even weekly. I believe that a manager should feel as close to his salespeople as if they were sharing the same office.

Besides spending time in the field with the reps, and seeing them at meetings or conferences, at least every three months I'd bring a group to our headquarters to spend a day with me. I knew what they did day to day, and I wanted them to get a sense of what I did and what goes on at corporate headquarters.

The branch office meeting is emphasized. While it has been mandatory to have a minimum of one per month, some branch managers hold meetings biweekly and even weekly.

IBM communicates with its sales force by providing terminals for them at the branch offices. In fact, IBM is one of the largest users of computers in the world. At the terminal, a rep can review new announcements; check on the status of orders; validate prices or terms; get information for an account, etc. The terminal also helps a rep sell by providing information about new product usage in a given industry. One salesperson might put into the system a message that describes a new solution to a problem. That information is now available to the entire organization. In effect, a central information data bank is available, where anyone can deposit or withdraw ideas, problems and solutions. A marketing rep also can keep up to date on his own annual quota status. He can see what he has to produce to meet his financial goals and how much a given transaction is worth to him.

The bigger an organization becomes, the harder its management must work at communication. Regardless of a company's size, I think, no more than eight to ten people should report directly to a single manager. This ratio assures each person of individual attention, without overburdening the manager. When a manager has too many individuals to supervise, it's almost impossible to maintain discipline and recognition. And of course nothing is more frustrating and demoralizing than to work for a manager who doesn't have adequate time for his staff.

IBM has a fundamental program that's designed to enhance communications as it boosts morale. The Executive Interview offers an employee a scheduled but rather informal conference with management one level above the person he or she works for. The idea is for the employee to know that someone other than his manager is aware of his accomplishments. The discussion is free-flowing, giving the employee every opportunity to express himself and to ask questions about the company and the business. This is very exciting to me because the program got started when Bob Woodworth, a very creative manager, came to me in the mid-sixties and outlined the need for enhanced employee communications. I immediately implemented the Executive Interview in my area of responsibility, the western United States. It was so successful that it became a valued addition to our companywide personnel programs. This program works because it's exercised: these things have to be more than good intentions to be meaningful.

I suppose every company has some form of 'Open Door' policy. At IBM, it's a basic communication channel, a policy that's deeply ingrained in the company's history. It's based on the conviction that every employee has the right to appeal the actions of those who are immediately over him or her in authority.

The employee is encouraged to discuss a problem with a manager or manager's manager, a personnel manager or the site manager. If a problem is not solved at that level, he can go to the president or the general manager of the division or subsidiary. Finally, if the employee isn't satisfied, he may cover the subject with the chief executive officer, either by mail or, if the CEO feels it is appropriate to the resolution, personally.

Some people outside IBM who know of this policy say, 'How can you make your CEO accessible to over 400,000 employees in this busy and complicated world of business?' How can you *not* be interested in what one person thinks or feels? These practices work because management believe in them, and most important, so does everybody else.

A Very Important Survey

Even though IBM does its best to see, hear, feel and understand the mind and mood of the sales force, it worries that something important might be missed. Every year, the total field force is required to answer a questionnaire (no signature is necessary) that asks such things as: Are you being challenged by your job? What work pressures do you have? Do you think IBM is still practicing respect for the individual? How do you evaluate your pay in light of your duties? What do you think about our pay compared with that in other companies? Are you satisfied with your career planning? How do you feel about headquarters management? Are they responsive to you? Are they providing you with enough tools to get the job done? How do you evaluate your manager? How do you evaluate your manager's manager?

This information is reviewed at each level of management, from the branch office to the summit. If a problem seems to have a pattern, action is taken.

At one time, the marketing reps' opinion of a particular division's management had dropped significantly. The complaints were justified. We gave the division president ninety days to get things turned around, or he would be replaced. We had to replace him.

The company always responds to the opinion surveys. A composite of what the reps say – pro and con – is distributed to everyone at branch office meetings, with management's reaction – pro and con. Most problems that surface are caused by managers who are unable to listen with understanding and communicate clearly. The key to an open and honest survey is voluntary participation coupled with a quick response from management.

In addition to the annual survey, every ninety days each sales rep and systems engineer answers a series of questions related to customer satisfaction: do the reps think the company is doing a good job? As a follow-up, IBM customers are surveyed by both the company and independent sources. An independent survey that does not inform the customer that IBM is the sponsor facilitates a candor that might not otherwise surface. Basically, the same questions are asked of the sales force and the customer, to see how well IBM people are tuned in to their accounts. These surveys help uncover both negative and positive trends.

There Is No Saturation Point in Education

The above words are etched in stone at the entrance to IBM's education center in Endicott, New York. Thomas Watson, Sr, believed that top management should spend 40 to 50 percent of its time educating and motivating its people, and this practice, handed down through Tom, Jr, has been carried on to the present.

It doesn't make sense to have a rep go through a one-year training program – no matter how thorough – and have it end there. Anyone who stops learning goes backward. Like any professional – from tax accountant to physician – an IBM representative must keep up to date with what's happening. This is particularly essential in so complex an industry as IBM's. It's not enough for marketing rep or systems engineer to know the new technological advances made by the company and by the information-processing industry. He must stay on top of what's happening in his area of specialization, whether it be banking, insurance, transportation or whatever. It's estimated that an experienced IBM marketing rep will spend fifteen days each year in the classroom, attending special industry schools and conferences.

Although there is no required reading list, considerable material is distributed to the field to be studied. Each week, the company announces an average of ten different products plus new programs, so the marketing people must deal with a continuous flow of information. All in all, it's estimated that 15 percent of their time is devoted to education.

In 1984, IBM had 42,000 managers and 1,500 people in executive positions throughout the world. In keeping with the idea that if it is important to train a person to sell, it is equally important to train a person to manage, the company promotes from within. Whatever a person's credentials, he or she must go through IBM's basic training program. An exceptional person could emerge as a management candidate in five years, but it takes an average person seven to ten years to make it.

A first-line manager receives eighty hours of classroom training during his first year on the new job. It's mandatory that within thirty days of his promotion, the new manager attend a one-week class at IBM's Management Development Center, a campus that occupies twenty-six acres of the corporate headquarters site in Armonk, New York. The program covers the company's history, beliefs, policies and practices, as well as basic managerial skills, including the motivation, appraisal and counseling of people. An emphasis is placed on strengthening employee-manager communications and keeping managers updated in a constantly changing environment. Flexibility is vitally important. A good manager must be able to adapt to change while preserving IBM's basic beliefs and philosophies. The material used in each class is this: 'Will it be useful next week, when the manager returns to his office?' Every year thereafter, the managers, all 42,000 of them, spend at least forty hours in the classroom.

There is also a Middle Managers' School, founded upon the recognition that special skills are needed to manage other managers. The classes concentrate on effective communications and people management, but also cover business concerns and strategies. Then, too, there are schools for the experienced middle manager and the senior manager. These deal with more sophisticated matters, such issues as external factors, both social and economic.

A company can't rely on executives to rise from its ranks by chance. It must be actively engaged in a continuous talent hunt. It's essential to find the very best people and prime them for future managerial positions. IBM's Executive Resources program seeks out and plans the careers of those who are considered to have especially high potential. All managers participate by identifying their superstars.

In another training program, promising young people are brought in as assistants to high-ranking company executives – one might be an assistant to the chairman's office, another to the president's office. After I had been with IBM for seven years, I served as administrative assistant to an executive vice-president, which gave me tremendous exposure and insight.

To broaden their perspective, future managers attend educational programs outside the IBM environment: the Menninger Clinic, Harvard's Advanced Management Program, the London School of Economics, MIT's and Stanford's Sloan Program. They may last from a week to a year. Those who excel attend the Advanced Managers' School, a program given in about forty colleges, including Harvard, Columbia, Virginia, Georgia and Indiana. IBM's highest-ranking executives may attend an executive seminar on federal government activities, given at the Brookings Institute, and a two-week international executive program is attended by the company's top two hundred executives. The program covers a broad range of subjects, from what's happening in South America and the Middle East, to the trade deficit and the federal budget. Topical events are studied with a special regard for their implications for the company today and in the future, and people like Henry Kissinger, Martin Feldstein and David Broder participate.

A few executives may enroll in the Aspen Institute of Humanistic Studies, which covers such diverse subjects as religion, astronomy and South American literature. Its purpose is to help the individual take a fresh look at his value system. It can activate a midlife awakening – stimulating ideas that haven't been considered for years.

IBM invests a lot of money in its people. Total estimated expenses for educating and training ran in excess of $600 million in 1984. But since the future of a company depends on the quality of its people, the investment is an imperative.

5

Future-Oriented Marketing

Sometimes the manager must perform with the courage and agility of a circus performer, carefully crossing the highwire between short-term problems and long-term objectives.

Marketing is the process used by an organization to relate creatively and productively to the environment in which it sells its products and services. *Effective* marketing requires the talent to speak in a language the marketplace understands; the insight and skill to find solutions to customers' problems; and the commitment to give value. To accomplish this, a company must be willing and able to use all its resources.

Remember that while selling tries to get the customer to want what you have, marketing tries to have what the customer wants. There is a fundamental difference between these two perspectives.

To IBM, marketing is a source of pride and joy. It is the vehicle upon which the company moves its goods, and it provides a voice that articulates what IBM is, what it believes in, and what it hopes to accomplish and contribute.

There's a lot to marketing — product planning, marketplace segmentation, pricing, distribution, advertising and promotion. Each of these requires the making of decisions based on assumptions about the future.

Shortsighted people deal almost exclusively with today's problems, programs, motivations and sales results. Of course, all these are tactically important, but well-managed companies keep looking ahead. They know that while today's actions are essential, the impact of these actions on the future must be predetermined.

The higher you are in management, the more important it is to think strategically. The responsibility of spelling out long-term strategies belongs to top management, who must make a clear statement on the importance of strategic planning and ensure that a long-range plan is in place – a plan that establishes definite goals. Everybody must be made aware of the impact of his daily activities on those long-term objectives.

My management style is based on the belief that while you are doing your best to get today's job done, a part of you must be aware of your influence on the future.

I have always told everyone who worked with me that I preferred them to spend more time on long-term matters than on day-to-day issues. What's needed are people who can conceptualize, who can visualize what's going to happen four and five years ahead.

You may decide today that by cutting your head count or reducing your advertising expenditures you can meet this quarter's goals and enhance the bottom line at the year's end, but you might regret it down the road. You'd better have a good fix on the future before implementing any immediate decision.

Balancing Act II

Sometimes the future-oriented manager must perform with the courage and agility of a circus performer, carefully crossing the highwire between short-term problems and long-term objectives.

A decision to invest in a project that cannot produce a quick profit can cause the decisionmaker to suffer migraine headaches, sleepless nights and more. The expenditures needed to get the new project off the ground will surely lower the current year's profit picture and possibly even have an adverse effect on the value of the company's stock. You must anticipate the reactions to all the negatives before putting the plan into motion. It takes a great deal of careful preparation, thoughtfully presented, to ward off potentially hostile stockholders who might try to climb the pole and cut the highwire before you make it across.

Many marketing managers give in too easily to the guardians of the bottom line. They'll squeeze every last sale out of a tired marketing program or product. They'll enjoy cheap sales for a short period because the start-up costs have long been amortized. For a while, fewer sales may produce a higher than usual profit margin, but the day of reckoning is certain to come. Before he knows it, the shortsighted marketing manager is faced with an eroding share of the market; his product, its packaging and the sales program are old and worn out, and he has nothing in the pipeline.

Of course, you want to get the most mileage out of your investments, but as with an automobile, you have to know when to tune them up, when to overhaul them and when to scrap them.

IBM is a master of balancing its long-term and short-term goals without sacrificing acceptable profit levels. If the information-processing industry grows to a trillion-dollar level in the 1990s, IBM, growing at the same rate, could be a $185 billion company.

Since 1979, IBM has invested about $13 billion in its factories to improve quality and reduce breakeven points. IBM spent $350 million to convert its twenty-five-year-old factory in Lexington, Kentucky, into one of the US's most automated plants. Before the plant was automated, labor accounted for about one third of manufacturing costs. Consistent with IBM's practice of job security, the company spent $5 million to retrain its Kentucky workers.

These massive investments – bets on the future – came during the 1970s, when IBM's growth rate (based on revenue) had slowed to about 13 percent. IBM pumped money back into the business in prodigious amounts. And it took some heat. One heard comments that IBM had lost its zip and was getting complacent. None of these criticisms, it turned out, was accurate. As an IBM financial expert said, 'The company took a short-term hit.' When you make such investments, there isn't a payback until the future. Well, the future has arrived.

The External Factors

No matter how well you plan ahead, there will always be unexpected external factors that you must deal with – changes in government regulations, politics, inflation, trade imbalances, unemployment, the prime rate . . . There may right now be on the drawing board government regulations that can make a product obsolete. When the EPA set clean-air standards, the automobile manufacturers had to invest billions of dollars switching to low-lead-gasoline-fueled cars; and oil companies had to make changes in their service station equipment as well as their gasoline production. When the prime rate rose to record heights, the housing industry, for one, was hit hard. Banking responded with variable interest rates and real estate developers switched from building single dwellings to building multifamily projects. President Reagan's grain embargo on Russia was an external factor that had a devastating impact on the small American farmer, who is especially vulnerable to external factors — government actions, natural disasters, banking practices, etc.

Women have created a series of problems and opportunities that most marketing departments are wrestling with today. In entering the work force en masse, women have changed their buying habits and what they consider their necessities. In the past, the automobile industry virtually ignored women as factors in marketing strategy. The industry can no longer turn its back on them, since women participate in 81 percent of all new car and truck purchase decisions. It's tougher now to market to women in the home, because fewer of them are home. On the other hand, mail order businesses are thriving because working women have less time to visit retailers during regular store hours. Of course, there are many more examples. Women must be reckoned with by marketing departments.

Sometimes an unexpected external factor can result from a company's own technology and marketing successes. Rapid technical enhancements made the computer available to almost every school, millions of homes and small businesses. Because so many people spend hours at the computer keyboard – and a lot of these people are children – the industry had to react to concern about the computer's effect on mind and body. In some European countries, governments are attempting to regulate such things as the height of keyboards and the clarity of video display terminals. IBM is dealing with these concerns and others now, although federal guidelines on visual display terminal (VDT) ergonomics standards are not presently anticipated.

An unexpected external problem in the computer field is the invasion of privacy by so-called hackers, who attempt to access confidential information. Unlawful access has become commonplace: people attempt to change their credit ratings, students alter grades, competitors steal secret data. For this reason, IBM offers its customers an option of new hardware and software features to protect their data. In the immediate future, I believe, the demand for this kind of security will be so high that it will be a major consideration in buying computer systems.

There are times when external factors may cause an organization to reevaluate itself top to bottom. At the end of the review, the company concludes that its best course of action is to go right on conducting business as usual – changes aren't necessary. This was what happened after the US Justice Department antitrust suit against IBM, filed in 1968, ended thirteen years later, in 1981, in what had become the longest such case in this country's history. Some 2,500 depositions were taken, and more than 66 million pages of documents were involved. IBM's former chairman Frank

Cary alone spent forty-five days making depositions and many more days preparing for them. As vice-president of marketing, I, too, spent days having depositions taken. Later, as the first IBMer called to testify at the trial, I again expended considerable time that could have been utilized more productively.

The government had charged IBM with attempting to monopolize the general-purpose computer market and sought to break up the company into smaller pieces, or at least change some of its practices. During this period, approximately twenty-five other suits were filed by competitors such as Greyhound, Memorex and Teletex, accusing IBM of utilizing its marketing practices to achieve what's referred to as 'a dominance of the marketplace'. Needless to say, we were distracted from the day-to-day job, and the time and money that went into such things as legal fees, paralegal people and preparation to protect ourselves was very costly. When it was all over, the Department of Justice completely vindicated IBM of any wrongdoing. The court had ruled: 'The suit was without merit.'

When the verdict was out, CEO John Opel said: 'IBM prevailed, first and foremost, because we were blameless. For all its efforts over those thirteen long years, the government failed completely to show any violation of that principle to which we adhere: IBM will not tolerate unfair or unlawful conduct anywhere in the business. That principle still stands. We'll continue to compete aggressively, as we always have, but always uncompromisingly within the letter and spirit of the law.' IBMers rejoiced because it had been proved that a corporation, regardless of its size, can achieve any level of penetration of a market as long as that penetration has been realized through excellence and fairness.

The case caused IBM to be very sensitive to the way it did business, and carefully analyze everything about itself. But in the end, IBM concluded that there was nothing to apologize for. The company had been conducting business at the highest ethical level, and reaffirmed its commitments to provide outstanding service and excellence in everything it did.

The antitrust suits filed against IBM illustrate that certain external factors can demand a great amount of a company's resources, but may not cause change. Nonetheless, you can't ignore the external factors around you, because they can have devastating consequences. Had IBM been found guilty of the antitrust charges, the law would have required the company to change substantially the way it did business. Yet IBM was so certain that it had done nothing wrong, a contingency plan was never prepared. Nor, during the thirteen-year period, did the case cause overreactions and changes in marketing practices that would have weakened IBM's position in the marketplace.

It is to be hoped that you never get involved in a long-drawn-out lawsuit that drains your resources of time and money. Even when a company wins the case, it ends up paying a high price. Yet, like every external factor you can't ignore, hoping it'll go away, you must give anything that turns up your absolute attention.

Each time an operating or a strategic plan is developed, a set of environmental assumptions should be made. You have to look down the road as far as you can and build as many safeguards as possible into your plans. Of course, you can't have contingencies in place for external factors that cannot be predicted. But you must have people who are sensitive to environmental changes, who can see beyond the confines of your business and can react quickly when confronted with the unexpected.

The Internal Danger Signs

If you are going to be able to manage people sensibly, you have to know what's happening *within* your own organization. Trouble may be brewing that won't be reflected in numbers alone. Probe around, talk, listen, observe your people: you find out by reading the signs. You have to be sensitive to mood changes and varying energy levels. *In Search of Excellence* calls it 'management by wandering around'. Maybe there are three resignations from one branch, or grumblings about inadequate recognition, or complaints about the size of raises.

A while ago, IBM suffered a higher-than-normal attrition in its sales force in Australia. Upon investigating the problem, IBM found that to speed up the ability to meet the demands in that country, the branch offices had been hiring a higher proportionate number of professional people as compared to university students. These experienced people left at a higher rate than usual, to work for other organizations within the information-processing industry. This abnormal voluntary attrition resulted from inadequate new employee orientation. They simply hadn't been exposed to IBM's culture.

A manager can observe many danger signs about an individual who works with him: There may be change in a person's physical appearance, level of concentration and attitude. These may accompany a drop in the person's productivity and the quality of his work. The number of customer calls made by a marketing rep takes a nosedive, or he may stay late at the office every night. You must find out what is causing this behavior. Is it something personal? Perhaps he's not getting along well with his spouse and doesn't want to go home. Or he may tell you, 'I haven't enough administrative people around here to support me, so here I am, filling out forms when I ought to be in front of the customer.'

For instance, a regional manager might notice that one of his branch managers is no longer spending the proper amount of time out in the field with his reps, meeting customers. Investigation might reveal that the reps are no longer inviting the branch manager to make calls because they feel he's lost touch with the marketplace.

There are countless internal danger signs, but you've got to put in the time to look for them. You have to be as sensitive to the people you pay as you are to the people you sell.

Changing Values

Civil rights. The Kennedy and King assassinations. Vietnam. Watergate. Women's liberation. Consumerism. The energy crisis. The events and movements of the past quarter century have caused America to reexamine its values and to initiate changes. A well-run marketing organization must be sensitive to what I call *forces of change*.

Because of these events and developments, people today are very concerned with the quality of their life.

Personal values are changing and IBM works at staying on top of those changes when making marketing and managing decisions. Changing attitudes about sex, marriage, family roots, religion, education and drugs have to be considered. People are more sophisticated, less trusting – thank goodness. They want to know what they're eating and what their kids are being taught and what things really cost. They're not as quick to buy Madison Avenue's pitch or blindly follow the fashion designers' bidding. For many, small really is beautiful.

Any company that doesn't think that these changing values are factors to be understood and dealt with is headed for trouble. Changing values is one of the reasons this country's growth rate in production began to slip in 1965, just when West Germany's showed a dramatic increase and Japan's began to soar. As you will well remember, it was the beginning of a decade of unrest throughout our country, and the workplace was certainly affected. Companies responded in different ways to the social changes. Some became as loosely structured and undisciplined as many sixties college campuses. IBM responded too – its change in relocation policies is an example – but it would not relent in its philosophical commitments to respect for the individual, service for the customer and excellence of performance. The result? IBM's productivity rate did not slip.

The Best Source of Information

The customer is perhaps your best source of information for long-term planning. After all, to survive, you must understand the customer's problems so you can provide solutions that withstand hard scrutiny over a period of time. Surveys and studies may be useful, but every small business can go directly to its customers for information. It's simple. Talk to them during your initial stages of planning. Ask for their opinions of designs, price and packaging. Involve them. Make them part of the decisionmaking process. It will make sense to them too. And keep going back to them as your plan progresses.

There are times when a customer enters into a Joint Study Agreement with IBM. After a nondisclosure compact is executed, IBM may install a preproduction prototype of a machine yet to be introduced to the marketplace. Customers help the company assess the new product's performance in a real-world environment. The customer benefits by having the product developed to fit his specific requirements.

On other occasions, IBM invites a dozen or so customers to a specific industry council – for example, top banking executives attend a Bankers' Council. Here customers critique IBM's practices and policies, as well as describe their needs and problems.

On a larger scale, IBM conducts what it calls industry conferences. Several hundred customers attend a convention at which the latest technology and most advanced applications are presented. The users share their experiences with one another. A company that has its customers working with other customers represents marketing at its finest.

A small company can't always afford to conduct a seminar or expect the top executives of a particular industry to attend. But a small industrial company could fly its top engineer, head of manufacturing and pricing manager to visit one or more of its leading customers. Most companies are satisfied to stay home, sit back and surprise their customers with new products or programs. What they miss by not taking the time to preview their plans could prove to be catastrophic. To their dismay, their new product may have missed the mark. Go to your customers and ask what they think their future needs are. You don't have to be shy or coy with them. Be direct. A small company that does this will get the information it needs. This is *not* an expensive venture, and the customer is complimented by the visit.

A New Opportunity – A New Product

Although IBM is supersensitive to movement in the marketplace and responds with new products with what I consider remarkable agility, you might be surprised at the company's studied approach to change. IBM has a large staff of people who study the marketplace in order to determine future needs of specific industries. This industry marketing unit, made up of former reps, systems engineers and professional hires, has in-depth knowledge of all aspects of a particular industry. It monitors the changes taking place in that industry, and speculates about the future.

IBM's marketing people are responsible ing the existing opportunities for new p various marketing division managers take of opportunities and submit what is called a Statement of Opportunity. In the document, a manager might predict that the retail industry is going to grow faster than the projected GNP rate. He'll supply as much data as possible to support his assumptions. His conclusion might be: 'More people will be buying. The graying of America will continue and the baby boom will expand.' Therefore, he might recommend that IBM put more dollars into products catering to retailers.

A typical report may include an explanation of perceived opportunity, analysis of the competitive environment, and a description of the product the manager thinks will sell.

IBMers refer to these situations as 'windows of opportunity.' That means: 'Urgent! We'd better get this out fast or somebody else will beat us to it.' Just how fast a company responds to a particular opportunity depends on how quickly its parts can react. And IBM is geared up to act, not just to react. Every department has to move – you can't afford to have anyone dragging his feet once the commitment is made and the time frame is set.

Once marketing identifies what they believe the new opportunity should be, the development and manufacturing staffs take over. Responsible for establishing specific product requirements, the technical staff is given the freedom to select the best technology to produce the product.

After a commitment is made to introduce a new product at some future date, additional marketing research determines just how receptive the marketplace will be. And before any dollars are actually allocated to production, a research study is done to support the initial assumptions and validate the product's practicability. Several checkpoints are established, the first perhaps three to six months after the product's conception. The plan is then reassessed by engineering, manufacturing, marketing and finance before funds are allocated for tools and parts. About ninety days later, the opportunities are reevaluated, this time by taking a hard look at the revenue and profit picture. With all costs known, before the product is actually manufactured another review establishes what is considered a realistic price. A formal review is then made by both line and staff to determine whether the original commitment is still valid. It's a continuous procedure from checkpoint to checkpoint, reevaluating and going on.

This may seem unnecessary, but I assure you that it's time and money well spent. It's a safeguard against manufacturing a product that makes little or no profit and has no reality in the marketplace. I can't emphasize enough how important it is to keep a formal dialogue and frequent checkpoints going throughout the stages of a product's development. This is nothing more than 'interlocking' all of a company's internal functions before the final release of the product to the marketplace.

IBM's recent entry into the personal computer field represents a different approach to its past marketing efforts.

I must tell you that the personal computer has been a marketing challenge for IBM. The product couldn't absorb the high costs of IBM's traditional marketing system, and forced the company to look at less expensive selling methods.

Off to a late start, with many competitors already in

the field, IBM established a task force to pursue the development and distribution of this new product. As it turned out, the personal computer opened up several new marketplaces for us – as well as new challenges. New markets included students, and people who use it in the home.

In order to effectively reach this vast number of potential buyers, a bold marketing decision was made. For the first time in the company's history, dealers would sell a significant volume of an IBM product. The real test was to find quality dealers who would let IBM educate and train them to perform at a level equal to its own sales force. After analyzing various industries, we concluded that IBM could make it work. By insisting that its beliefs about sales and service be respected and adhered to, IBM felt certain that the dealers selected would live up to the commitment IBM made to its customers. The goal was that customers would not see a difference between doing business with IBM and buying from its dealers.

To accomplish this, every support function had to be examined. It was vital for the company to provide the consumer with immediate service. The consumer needed convenient locations where his personal computer could be dropped off for servicing, in addition to the option of IBM service at his own site. From some remote areas, a customer would have to ship his personal computer to a central maintenance depot. The proper service strategy was as necessary as an effective selling strategy.

IBM established a series of education programs that not only trained the dealers on the product itself but taught them better ways to manage their people and their dollars. And finally IBM developed its first consumer advertising campaign.

This new opportunity has presented IBM with a continuous flow of challenges that have kept our people excited and busy.

The Little Tramp

IBM never advertised widely to attract new prospects until the introduction of the personal computer, so its experience in this area was limited. I think the Charlie Chaplin character as spokesman for the IBM PC was a stroke of brilliance by the advertising agency. The 'Little Tramp' personifies the qualities the company wants to project for the new product – uncomplicated, unintimidating and fun.

Traditionally, IBM's corporate advertising program has been institutional in nature. An overall corporate point of view was projected to a general audience: 'The computer is something to want, not fear.' 'Our products make life easier for you; we have educational applications, and solutions for your business problems.' 'Here is IBM, and we're involved in a variety of products and services, all providing some benefit for you.'

Appearing in newspapers, national magazines and on television (IBM was a major sponsor of the 1984 Olympics, and such specials as *The Nutcracker* and *A Christmas Carol*), the ads have been designed to create goodwill and promote the company as a worthy corporate citizen. The audience is told that IBM products are of the finest quality; that IBM people have been trained to give the best service; that the company is innovative and caring, solution-oriented and responsive – not some gray, monolithic giant. IBM wants everyone to know that it cares about its customers and people who work for it; that it has a sense of humor and, above all, is approachable.

Product advertising, on the other hand, mainly zeroes in on a specific market, perhaps focusing on a particular piece of equipment. It's more 'hard sell' and aims at generating the interest to buy. These solution-oriented advertisements often appear in 'vertical' media such as trade and business publications, including *American Banker*, *Petroleum Week*, *Chemical Week* and *Aviation Week*. However, like the corporate advertising, they also appear in 'horizontal' media, including the *Wall Street Journal*, the *New York Times*, *Fortune*, *Business Week*, *Time* and *Newsweek*.

In the past, when IBM's business was strictly marketed by its blue-suit organization and a medium-sized computer had a price tag in the hundreds of thousands of dollars, advertising was used almost exclusively to support the sales force. No attempt was made to move products the same way automobiles or appliances are sold. Corporate advertising in horizontal media almost always promoted the company flag rather than specific products. It wasn't until the 1980s, when technological advances lowered computer prices and broadened the marketplace, that IBM beefed up its product advertising budget, and focused on promoting sales of the personal computer.

The majority of the company's revenues, however, have always come from larger systems, sold by marketing reps, which are only minimally helped by advertising. Until the scope of the market was expanded by alternatives to the traditional distribution system, it didn't make much sense to do a great deal of advertising, even for smaller items like typewriters, copiers and work stations. IBM wasn't geared then to take advantage of the prospects a national advertising campaign would attract. Now the advertising has changed. The company is no longer limited to the one-on-one selling of reps; and can also count on IBM Product Centers, independent dealers, catalogs and the telemarketing program.

I do not doubt that advertising is an effective stimulator. It piques a prospect's curiosity and provokes him to make a phone call or go looking for a product. It's a terrific support for a selling force – who can close orders with fewer calls – and since an industrial call can cost almost three hundred dollars, effective advertising is a welcome aid.

IBM doesn't view advertising as an expense but as an investment in increased sales productivity. Helping the sales departments to keep pace with the manufacturing department's ability to turn out products, advertising speeds up inventory time and shortens the selling cycle.

Surveys have proved that IBM's advertising has successfully created new customers at the retail outlet. To a seven-city survey that asked customers what had brought them into the stores, 46 percent of respondents replied that it was advertising and direct mail. In Baltimore, as a four-month test market, expenditures on local advertising were increased to two and one half times the going rate. Store traffic and sales more than doubled. So advertising at IBM is no longer considered simply a tool to assist the sales force; it is a marketing tool to generate orders.

IBM attempts to decentralize its advertising as much

as possible. Typically, international companies have a global advertising campaign, created at their corporate headquarters and disseminated around the world, translated into the language of each country where they conduct business. IBM's ads have a different look in each country. For example, IBM Germany and IBM United Kingdom have the freedom to run their own product advertising, subject to an overview from European headquarters in Paris, where IBM standards of professionalism, honesty and quality are monitored.

In compliance with IBM's emphasis on fairness, the advertising focuses on selling the merits of products and services. While it may be in vogue today to knock the competition, IBM disagrees with the tactic. Just as marketing reps are not permitted to disparage a competitor, neither is the advertising department. Personally, I avoid doing business with companies whose advertising message is what's wrong with the competition.

Of course, advertising isn't worth a nickel if you don't have the distribution system to make the products readily available. And it's not worth much, in the long run, if the products you're selling and the service you're providing are inferior.

The Contention System

In a mom-and-pop operation, mom argues that they should do this and pop argues that they should do that. And if they don't settle on what to do between themselves, they go to a third party (a son-in-law, their accountant, etc.) to aid their decisionmaking.

On a more formal basis, IBM does the same thing.

The corporation encourages debate and a multiplicity of views. If staff and line don't agree, for example, they'll try to thrash it out until they come to some sort of meeting of minds. To keep people from getting their way by winning a shouting match, the divergent points of view are carefully documented. On occasion, I had heated debates with division presidents about the allocation of marketing resources, and whether we had too many or too few people. Through our management system, the differences were eventually resolved by a formal committee of top-ranking IBM officers. Happily, a lot of arguing is done at IBM – about new products, changes in pricing, revisions of terms and conditions, restructuring of the organization and overall long-term objectives.

Depending on the subject and its importance, IBM's contention system can go all the way up the organization and require different parties to meet in the boardroom with the president and/or chairman, who presides over the debate. As marketing head, I might want a new product to be developed and ready for market by a given date in order to meet competition. The engineering head might disagree, believing that a new product wasn't even needed, that the enhancement of an existing product would do. Each of us would present his views, and top management would serve as arbitrator. In a case of this nature, a clear-cut decision in favor of one view could be made, or a compromise suggested. Or the response could be: 'You're both wrong. Go back and do your staff work.'

One of the real values of this sort of contention system is that while people may disagree, they don't have to compromise themselves in order to settle an issue. At IBM, it is called the 'right of nonconcurrence'.

Once a decision is made, there's no animosity. It's not a game of win or lose; everybody is playing on the same team. Both line and staff are held accountable for the final results.

Shifting Gears

Businesses as well as entire industries have fallen by the wayside because they failed to perceive themselves correctly. The example most frequently cited is the buggy whip industry, which failed to realize it was in the transportation business; and as we all know, the movie industry almost suffered a knockout blow when television hit the scene in the 1950s. It took at least a decade for the moguls to realize that they were in the entertainment business and stop perceiving themselves as filmmakers whose products had to be viewed in theaters. This is Ted Levitt's thesis, highlighted in his classic article, 'Marketing Myopia,' which appeared in the *Harvard Business Review* in 1960.

A business can suffer other forms of myopia. It can bask in the luxury of its own success. Of course, a company that slows down and rests on its laurels is headed for trouble.

Back in the fifties, when IBM was considered the leader in the information processing industry, Tom Watson, Jr, boldly led the company from the world of punch cards to the world of stored programming. I was fortunate to be among its marketing pioneers. A small group of us attended one of the first commercial electronic data processing schools, to be trained away from the old concepts. From a technical as well as a marketing point of view, this was a drastic change in direction. It was perhaps the most significant change in the company's history.

In 1964, after investing $5 billion, IBM announced a new family of computers, called the System/360. The retooling investment was huge. The new product would not be compatible with IBM's existing systems. Talk about risk! At the time IBM was ready to make the move, its 'old' product accounted for well over half of IBM's revenue and profit. New programming required new skills. IBM customers could have rejected the company's new baby and converted to the competition. To many, it was a foolish gamble. Some doubting IBMers dubbed the program 'You Bet Your Company'. Cynics cried out, 'If it ain't broke, don't fix it.' It certainly would have been easier to stick with a successful product. But enough visionaries believed that standing still was equivalent to going backward.

The most insidious disease in business is complacency. People reflect too long on their accomplishments. Success is fleeting and should never be expected to last forever. As you work to retain it, you continue to seek new opportunities. Pioneering is risky, but business myopia is riskier. A successful company doesn't wait for outside influences to shape its destiny. It looks ahead. It asks itself 'What if?' questions: 'What if there's inflation?' 'What if there's a recession?' 'What if the competition does this?' It might not always come up with the right answers, but it's rarely taken by complete surprise.

While the computer industry is highly volatile and constantly changing, IBM is sometimes characterized as a great big monolith, never experiencing disruption. The company has been compared to a snowball rolling downhill, getting bigger and bigger. I assure you this is not an accurate assessment.

It's easy to look at the present company and think that everything simply fell into place. However, had the company failed to read the tea leaves, the IBM the world knows today would be a far different organization. IBM, like any company, has not been impervious to external factors and internal upheavals; both Watsons adhered to the principle: 'We will change everything about our corporation. We will alter our terms and conditions, we will change our organization and its products. We will change our policies. We will do whatever is necessary to keep our people challenged and motivated; to assure that we have the money to invest in people, research and development; and to give our customers the best possible value. We will change everything except our beliefs.'

Obviously, IBM hasn't shied away from making major changes when necessary. I mentioned the switch from keypunch card to stored programming products. Another bold marketing change was made in 1969, when IBM switched from selling its products in a 'bundle' (one price purchased all components in a package) to pricing components separately and allowing the customer to pick and choose. IBM began to unbundle at a hectic time, when several new domestic competitors as well as the Japanese were entering the market, and it took two years to implement. It would have been easier to make this change in calmer waters. But that simply wasn't IBM's style in making hard decisions. Most important, from a customer point of view, the time was right for change.

In 1981, IBM made a major overhaul in its marketing

structure. Three divisions had been selling IBM products: one handled typewriters, copiers and word processing equipment; another sold only small and medium-sized computers; and the third sold large computer systems. Reps often called on the same customers, causing an overlap of proposals and activities. When customers became confused, IBM began to consider alternatives.

Consequently, the three divisions were merged into two. The National Accounts Division sold the full product line to the top two thousand IBM customers, and the National Marketing Division sold the full product line to a wider customer base, ranging from small offices to major accounts not assigned to NAD.

At the time of these changes, IBM was enjoying prosperous times and some thought it was a mistake to rock the boat. And it would have been far easier to let the complaints slide. But we knew that the reorganization would enable IBM to give better service to its customers and to optimize our resources, so the company went ahead with it. It was a massive undertaking to reeducate our salespeople and match skills with customer needs. And it took incredible resolve for those in the field to adjust to the new demands. It was not a painless changeover and there were risks. But it was a thoughtful gamble that worked. IBM's sales volume and net profits have since reached record highs.

As a further example of meeting the needs of an ever-changing marketplace, in January 1986, IBM merged and then geographically split these two US divisions to form the North-Central Marketing Division and the South-West Marketing Division. Each field office now sells the full product line to all companies, regardless of size, within its geographic area. IBM has never been afraid to revamp its marketing organization, with each change being right for the time.

New Channels of Distribution

One of IBM's most intellectually challenging, exciting and difficult changes has been the development of alternate channels of distribution. Throughout the company's history, products were always sold via the direct interface of marketing reps and systems engineers. Even so, the challenge for any company is to make its sales force even more productive, and to deploy them as intelligently as possible.

The introduction of the personal computer and other low-cost products dictated new and complementary approaches to the basic IBM selling and installation approach. A broad distribution system had to reach more customers than ever before – at competitive prices. IBM set out to be not only the low-cost producer but the low-cost seller as well.

Corporate marketing was asked to review what was happening throughout the industry and recommend a course of action. This study analyzed our direct mail, telephone selling and other marketing programs. We visited and conferred with companies that utilized dealers and distributors outside the computer industry.

One key factor was the forecast that by 1988 approximately 35 percent of the total industry's information-processing revenue would be generated from nontraditional sales approaches. Clearly we needed to move quickly, since only a very small percentage of IBM's future revenue was expected to come from these new techniques.

I presented this scenario at a top management conference in Woodstock, Vermont. From there, Frank Cary and John Opel didn't hesitate to tell the line executives to initiate creative actions and establish a dual marketing strategy. We would continue to enhance our existing branch office structure, but at the same time expedite the use of a complementary network of distribution channels.

In 1983, the National Distribution Division was formed to sell high-volume, low-cost products through alternate distribution channels. Besides the approximately one hundred IBM Product Centers in the US, an increasing number of retail stores and independent dealers are selling IBM products. In addition, there are hundreds of companies that buy IBM products, add substantial value to them, usually in the form of software or additional hardware, and resell them to customers. In 1984, there were approximately 10,000 dealer outlets worldwide selling selected IBM products.

IBM is also reaching thousands of potential customers through catalogs and direct mail campaigns. With its toll-free telephone number for selected customer orders, IBM Direct receives ten thousand calls daily, generating a revenue flow that amounts to several million dollars a day.

The results have been impressive. In 1984, sales through nontraditional channels accounted for a growing percentage of IBM's total revenue. But it hasn't been easy. First of all, marketing representatives were worried about their future role. At our recognition events and other meetings, we constantly had to reassure them. No way did we want to turn our representatives against the channels of distribution or the channels against our marketing force.

Some problems still exist where IBM's field force initiates the interest, then the customer goes to a Computerland, Businessland, Sears Roebuck or other dealer to buy the system. Progress is being made and most of the problems have been overcome. In addition to changing IBM's thinking, the experience has affected pricing practices and made the company more competitive.

We live in a changing world and the future cannot be predicted with certainty. That's an obvious statement, but how we deal with change and the future is not so obvious. Change can be an ally when your company is alert and sensitive and has its antennae reaching in all directions, picking up all the signals around you. Of course, change will be your enemy if it catches you by surprise. You must control change – or change will control you. To the fearful, change is threatening. They know that things will somehow get worse. The hopeful have faith that change will make things better. But to those special people who love a challenge and are 'light on their feet', change is stimulating and exciting. They are the people who can make a difference. They can make a company. The people who make things happen are in demand and should be guarded jealously. Those who watch things happen and those who aren't sure what's happening are left behind.

Occurrence Management

Managers who fail to understand the potential that modern technology offers will fall by the wayside in this highly competitive world. The requirement is not to convert people into technologists, but rather to have a sense of awareness of what these devices can and cannot do.

We are finally reaching a stage in our society when computer technology in the hands of truly creative people is being used as it's meant to be: *to amplify man's intelligence and provide a business life-style that is more rewarding and productive.* For the foreseeable future, there will be a continual flood of paperwork and administrative trivia, and a need to communicate better. This dictates the need to simplify the information flow and separate out that which is important. Having visited organizations all over America during the past several years, I have observed that progressive managers no longer want to deal with information of a historical nature – other than to look at the past for its heritage value. Today the emphasis is on what I call *occurrence management*, which concentrates on identifying a potential problem and taking action before it happens. It also requires concentrating on your organization's strength. If a product is selling well in Dallas but poorly in Seattle, you go to Dallas to find out what they're doing right, not to Seattle to find out what's wrong. A computer system can be the tool to help accomplish this.

Modern technology also enables a business to effectively identify who, within its own organization, is the best source of information. For this reason, many companies are switching from a vertical style of management to a horizontal one — which I have always preferred. I never cared where a person was in the management hierarchy, but went to whoever I felt could provide me with the most timely and accurate response. I respected the individual's intellect and capability.

6

Solution-Minded Selling

People buy products for what they can do,
not for what they are.

When I'm asked, 'What products does IBM sell?' I answer, 'IBM doesn't sell products. It sells solutions.' The answer may sound kind of flip, but its meaning is quite serious. People buy products for what they can do, not for what they are. They buy products to solve problems. If a person's problem is straight straggly hair, when the fashion is a halo of ringlets, the solution may come in the form of a curling iron, plastic rollers, a chemical compound or a visit to a hair stylist. It's not the product that is important to the buyer; the solution to the problem is what matters. All the buyer wants is curly hair.

The information processing business is all problem solving and solution selling. If I call on you, I try to convince you that I can make your job easier, improve your cost structure and help you provide better service for your customers, and I'll probably get your attention. But one thing you can count on: I'll never try to sell you a typewriter, a copier or a computer. An IBM marketing rep's success depends totally on his ability to understand a prospect's business so well that he can identify and analyze its problems and then come up with a solution that makes sense to the customer. Don't be surprised if that solution involves an IBM system, but it doesn't always. It might involve reprogramming the existing equipment or buying a new set of application packages. You can be sure, though, that there will be no attempt to 'sell' a piece of equipment that isn't an integral part of a solution.

I said the rep has to know the customer's business in order to understand his problems; he also has to know his own product line if he is going to be of any help to the customer. And he has to know what the competition has to offer – its quality, pricing, delivery, etc. The people in the field have to be a combination of analyst, consultant, applications specialist, technologist and salesperson – and they have to be good in every area. Too many companies think of their reps only as salespeople, their primary and perhaps only function being to persuade a prospect to buy their product. If the prospect doesn't need the product, the salesperson is expected to create an illusion of need – then get the money and run before reality settles in. That's not IBM's approach.

Today's salesperson has to be a lot more to the customer than a genial, back-slapping, joke-telling Willy Loman type, who drops in each season to entertain and show his wares. He's performing best when he really understands the concept of solution selling.

You Can't Get an *A* if You Don't Do Your Homework

I've never known a successful salesperson who doesn't do his homework before he calls on a customer.

It goes without saying that the rep should know his product line like the back of his hand. How, otherwise, can he relate his products to customers' needs? A company that sends an improperly trained salesperson into the field is insulting its customers and wasting their time.

I go further than that – I think it's just as bad to call on a customer without first giving that customer some serious thought and study.

Your particular business may determine what kind of information you'll find helpful. But almost any rep will benefit from scanning the customer's annual report and 10K – especially if it's a new customer or a prospect.

As IBM's marketing vice-president, I reviewed the action file that is kept on every key IBM customer before I made a call. I couldn't imagine walking in cold, thinking I'd just wing it. I do just the same kind of homework when speaking to a group of customers at an industry conference. My staff helps me get information from the field so I can speak to the problems of my audience. Just as I don't believe in canned sales pitches, I don't believe in canned speeches. I don't think they ring true.

It's important to update yourself regularly on even those customers you've known for years. Recently I made a call on a very large insurance company that I hadn't been to for quite some time. Although I knew the company well, I spent a half hour reviewing its latest 10K and annual reports. The thirty minutes were well spent. I learned of three recent major investments, and of some significant reorganization that I hadn't heard about. During the course of my conversation with some of the insurer's top executives, my homework paid off. They were flattered that I knew what was going on and that I cared enough to remember the 'numbers' involved in their recent acquisitions.

I had learned enough in the half hour of homework to know that their expansion would involve challenges that IBM could help with right from the outset.

It doesn't matter who the customer is; you're paying him a wonderful compliment when you demonstrate that you know something about his business – information that required research and thought. This approach is head and shoulders above the salesperson who walks in off the street and says, 'I was in the neighborhood and thought I'd drop in.'

Once you get your foot in the door, it takes more than a look at the prospect's annual report to win his business, especially when you're up against stiff competition. Years ago, I was asked by a marketing rep to join him in making a visit to a multibillion-dollar bank. We had our work cut out for us. The bank claimed that it was satisfied with its existing equipment, installed by one of our competitors – and to make matters even more difficult, the competitor's president sat on the bank's board of directors.

We did our homework well. Our strategy was to demonstrate unconditionally that our people were solution-oriented. That they were knowledgeable in the banking field. That we had the expertise to serve the bank's present and future needs. That IBM's marketing and engineering organizations were equipped to anticipate the banking industry's problems and needs during the next five to ten years. We worked hard to prove that we could be an important asset to them. I made more than a dozen calls on the bank over a period of several months, and during that time, arranged for its people to visit with other leading banks around the country to see firsthand how we perform. Then we took them to our education centers and said, 'These are the people who will come to you and train your staff in preparation for the installation of the IBM equipment. This is just the beginning of our partnership with you and the commitment we will make.'

We made it obvious that our interest went far beyond the sale of equipment. It was important that the bank executives meet with our product planners and highly skilled engineers, to convey their views and to get to know the people who would modify our equipment to meet their needs, if necessary. They were impressed that we would come to their premises and set up an entire education program for their people – top to bottom. They were impressed, too, with the banking knowledge of our systems engineers, who were thoroughly trained in the particular products the bank would need. We convinced them that our specialists would be on hand with solutions to whatever problems could occur. No area was left unexplored. We demonstrated that we not only knew where their industry was headed but could fully see its future needs. We got the business, because we sold them our people and their ability to solve problems – and convinced them that we were much more than just a producer of business machines. Like the person with straight straggly hair, they wanted their problems solved and didn't care if the solution came in a bottle or a crate.

Role-Playing the Customer

IBM has a two-week course for its sales force that requires the marketing rep to role-play an IBM customer. Conducted with Harvard, it's called the President's Class. Here the salesperson is confronted with a series of problems and conditions a customer might face. The purpose is to help the marketing people understand how an executive thinks and what he does on a day-to-day basis.

Every organization can put its salespeople through a similar exercise. Role-playing requires only two people – they can alternate as a customer and salesperson. One successful real estate agency I know has its trainees alternately play agent and customer, actually showing each other through homes. Experienced salespeople hired by the firm from competitive realtors and put through the role-playing exercise have realized how different the perspective became when they walked in the shoes of a potential buyer.

Of course, every customer is different, so a rep must learn to put himself in many pairs of shoes.

Many times the most direct way to get to a customer's problem – and often the only way – is to listen to him. Asking penetrating questions and listening to the answers: what could be simpler? Unfortunately, few people know how to listen, and salespeople are no exception. It's a major deficiency in our whole communication system, and our private, professional and public lives suffer because of it. I don't mean to get on a soapbox, but I think that it's a weakness in our educational system not to have courses in listening, and make the passing of them a requirement for graduation. The idea that the supersalesperson is a glib, fast-talking peddler is a complete misconception. The best professional salespeople are the best listeners. They know the importance of giving the customer time to think through and then verbalize his problems and concerns. It's important not only because the rep will learn a lot, but because it's flattering to the customer, who becomes an ally. Instead of the rep being the aggressor and the customer the defender of his pocketbook (and his eardrums), the two work together at defining and solving a problem. If they are both successful, a sale will be made. If the salesperson wasn't able to contribute to the solution, he didn't deserve to make the sale. And if his listening skills are weak, he's starting off with a handicap.

Specialization – The Only Way

IBM's customer list covers many different industries, and because a number of its products and programs can be tailor-made to handle specific tasks, it's imperative to build a sales force of industry specialists. It's imperative, that is, if the intention is to run a solution-minded business. A salesperson can't be expected to be an authority on the automobile industry *and* the textile industry *and* the shipping industry. No matter how competent, he or she simply cannot call on a bank and talk about demand deposits and trust accounting, and then meet with an industrial company across the street to discuss an inventory or engineering problem.

As anyone in business knows, it's a full-time job to be expert in one field – to understand its problems, decode its jargon, bring direction and fresh ideas to its future. So IBM specializes. There are fifteen major industry classifications, and each has subdivisions. In transportation, there are specialists in airlines, motor freight and railroads. In retailing, there are department store and supermarket specialists. In banking, there are savings and loan specialists and finance specialists. These people zero in on their specialty as if they were going to become a leader in that industry – as if they were going to become a banker or run a railroad. When calling on their customers, they bring expertise and insight that a salesperson who is strictly a product-seller could never bring.

Some companies think this procedure is too expensive. It's true that several of your people might be driving down the same highway, headed for the same city – one to call on an insurance company, one to see a grocery chain, another to visit an airplane plant. The quality of work accomplished by the specialists more than pays for the added expenses.

In the large metropolitan areas, IBM branch offices are organized by industry to service their market. Where there are several branches, each has its own specialization. Training centers specialize in a particular industry and are involved in education programs at various universities. Years ago, I established a program at Rutgers University for our banking specialists. I chose Rutgers because it was one of the best banking schools, where the bankers send their people for special training. The program focused on what's new in the banking industry. It gave our people a better view of the important issues facing top banking executives.

Several hundred experts in division headquarters work with the field people, assisting them with industry applications. These specialists design applications and implement systems for a cross-section of American business. One might go to a particular city with a marketing rep to consult with a customer who has a serious inventory control problem. With a true understanding of his business, he can evaluate the problem and design a solution.

One Houston branch specializes in the petroleum industry and has a team of specialists who work only in the area of mining. When they designed a large system for a major seismic petroleum concern, it also became *the* system for the mining industry. Specialization by industry isn't only for large corporations. Many smaller companies, out of necessity or choice, serve a single industry. These organizations may not have the manpower and financial resources to do otherwise, but by becoming experts in servicing a particular industry they may, in time, become recognized as the leaders in their field and build a terrific business around this reputation.

Showcasing a Customer

IBM relies heavily on its customers to help its marketing efforts — especially those customers that are considered to have leadership roles in their industry. IBM *showcases* these customers whenever it can. In a business like IBM's, most of the creative effort takes place in the field. The customers are the real innovators and their premises often are IBM's laboratory. It's up to IBM's marketing people to share their successes with other customers.

Sometimes, no matter how much time and effort a marketing rep puts into describing his products and services, making a truly outstanding presentation, the prospect still can't comprehend the end result. The best solution is to visit a successful customer installation. A satisfied customer speaking in your behalf is an ideal endorsement. It means a great deal when he tells your prospect: 'Here's what we are accomplishing from this program. Here is the improved application. Here is the improved productivity. This is the savings we realized. This is the end result.'

For the most part, customers are delighted to cooperate. Of course, don't expect an oil company to show a leading competitor a new mathematical model that finds oil in the ground! Nor will an automobile manufacturer in Detroit agree to showcase one of its IBM engineering display terminals containing model designs for the next three years.

The future-oriented marketing industry conferences I have mentioned are in part an extension of this idea of showcasing. Industry leaders attend these IBM-sponsored conferences at their own expense, and enthusiastically share their experiences with other companies in their industry. The conferences include sessions of special interest to financial, personnel, legal and marketing executives, but most exciting and effective is when these prestigious leaders describe their problems and share their solutions with everyone else. It's incredibly important to IBM, since it was, in most cases, a partner in finding the solution.

The Bits and Bytes

Since IBM is very serious about selling solutions, not products, its marketing reps don't try to dazzle their clients or prospects by dumping a lot of technical jargon on them. That doesn't mean that they're ignorant of the technology behind the products that implement the solutions. They're not like the car salesman who told me, 'Look, I don't know what's under the hood. I'm not a mechanic. If I talked about gear ratios and horsepower, I'd scare people away.'

I don't buy that line about not needing the technical knowledge. IBM's marketing reps spend months learning about their products and they're regularly updated throughout their careers, learning more and more about bits and bytes. If a salesperson doesn't know the latest specifics about his product, how can he understand its application for solving the customer's problem?

However, a salesperson is only as good as his ability to describe his product so that a customer can understand it. While understanding its bits and bytes is vital, he must also know how much information is useful to the customer. An engineer might have a keen interest in a computer system's basic technology. He's likely to ask about its capacity to switch information at a millisecond or microsecond rate. On the other hand, if you're talking to the company's chief financial officer, he's more interested in the end result: the application of the machine. You must be able to walk both lines – knowing when selling the bits and bytes is appropriate. Too much technical detail can dilute the selling effort.

A salesperson entering the field could become smitten with the jargon, but it doesn't take long for him to realize the importance of using 'computer talk' sparingly. To me, people who fill their conversation with foreign phrases come off as affected snobs – and that includes technical jargon.

A Constant Search

At IBM, it's often said: 'Nothing is successfully sold until it's successfully installed. Nothing is ever installed until it's properly sold.' *Sell – Install:* the two words go together, never one without the other. When an initial sale is consummated, it is generally for a specific application. Two or three applications at most. But the sale doesn't end there. The delivery and installation phase of a sale might take as long as a year; meanwhile the customer must be educated in applying the product properly. IBM is constantly working with its customers, always trying to find new applications to further justify the equipment.

For instance, a marketing rep sells a piece of IBM equipment to the chief financial officer of a manufacturing firm, to handle its payroll. Later, he meets with the company's engineering and manufacturing people, and finds that with the same equipment they can speed up the orders on the shop floor and improve the inventory turnover. And when he talks to the people in purchasing, he learns that it takes five days to process those purchase orders. The processing time might be cut dramatically with minor additions to the existing machine: another disk drive, or additional tapes, or maybe another printer. The point is, a good marketing rep makes an ongoing effort to find new applications for the customer's equipment. The more problems uncovered and the more solutions, the greater the company's value to the customer.

I don't believe in trying to do too much at first with a new account. It's better to start off with a single application, as in payroll or accounts receivable, and demonstrate how the equipment will perform. My advice to a new account has been to do things gradually, justify the equipment on one or two applications. Once it is demonstrated that this is right for the customer, with no disruption in his business, *then* IBM will move forward with additional applications. Over the years, I have found that when you try to have a solution for everything right away, you tend not only to overpromise but to overwhelm the customer.

A computer system often has the guts of a customer's business tied up in it. Anything that could go wrong with it must be anticipated, so it can keep performing around the clock, 365 days a year. As with the space shuttle, redundancies are built in to minimize any problems. But it gets back to a sale not being successful until the equipment is satisfactorily installed and working. IBM is in a repeat business, and *must demonstrate value every day*.

I have often said that each proposal must be cost-justified from the customer's point of view. But there are factors involved that can't always be controlled. For example, a product like the personal computer or System/36 will free up some time on your calendar or perhaps allow your administrative people and secretaries to get more done in less time, but unless that 'extra' time is used productively, the proposal doesn't save the customer money.

The values of some applications are more difficult to quantify than those of others. It's easy to justify an inventory control application. That's something tangible that you can put a dollar figure on. In the airlines industry, nothing is more perishable than an airplane seat. If it can be proved that a computerized reservations system will help fill those empty seats, that's tangible and cost-justifiable. On the other hand, handling more reservations in less time and responding to inquiries more quickly are intangible benefits. While the airlines know that they're providing a convenience for their customers, they can't measure an exact value received. I think it's always more difficult to cost-quantify an intangible reason for making a buying decision, but that is not to say a real value doesn't exist.

Finding new applications isn't limited to the computer industry, nor is growing with your customer base. Every salesperson should sell conservatively in securing the initial order. What's important is *getting the business*, and then performing so outstandingly that your customer will never go elsewhere to solve his problems.

Value-Added Selling

In today's competitive business world, product superiority alone isn't enough for making it in the marketplace. Firms with inferior merchandise are destined to fail, of course, but I've also seen companies collapse even though they had fine products. They knew they had a superior product and didn't take their competition seriously. You should assume your competition also has a good product and that you must

offer something extra. At IBM, this is referred to as
value-added selling.

Value-added selling comes in many forms. It's often
the difference that separates great organizations from
the rest of the pack. The quality of a product should be
the tip of the iceberg. I preach that 'The actual sale
doesn't begin until after the equipment has been
installed.' This means what you do for the customer
after he's signed on the dotted line is every bit as
important as what you did to earn the sale.

Value-added selling is why IBM was able to convince
the major bank I mentioned earlier to use our computer systems. We demonstrated in no uncertain terms
that we would do much more than just sell them
machines: we had the qualified people to meet their
long-term needs; we would educate their people, and
together we'd come up with innovative applications
on an ongoing basis. They *knew* that once our equipment was installed, it was only the beginning of a
long-term partnership.

Not every company can go to such great lengths to
win accounts with value-added selling, but I sincerely
believe that every organization must somehow convey
some added value in what it does — perhaps an important convenience or service or guarantee.

It's not always the company that offers the 'best
deal' pricewise that does the most business. I once
bought a car because the dealer convinced me that he'd
give me an outstanding service. As I was looking at
some of the models in the showroom, he said, 'While
you're here, I want you to walk through our service
department with me. See how clean it is. See the
working habits of our people. I want you to see the
large parts inventory we have, so you'll know that if

something goes wrong, we're not going to say, "This job will take about three weeks." I also want you to meet our service manager. He's been with us for fifteen years.' Not that the price of the car wasn't a factor. It was. But I was impressed with how the dealer showed me the total resources available to me. I liked the pride he and his people had in their organization. They made me feel good about putting my confidence in their ability to give dependable service.

In this case, the value added made the difference. I don't care what the product is – it's what you offer over and above the basic product and how you perform that builds a solid business.

Many companies do have excellent support functions, but too often their people fail to let the customer know what's available. If my auto dealer hadn't coordinated his service department's and his sales force's efforts, I wouldn't have known what added value I was getting when I bought my car. Support functions such as IBM's education and office systems centers won't do anyone much good unless they are utilized by all systems engineers and all marketing reps with their customers.

Everything IBM does is influenced by its effort to excel in value-added service. If a customer is lost, you can bet it's not because of IBM's apathy or smugness. And you can also bet that IBM takes its competition seriously. If they intend to take away a customer, they'll have to care about that customer as much as IBM does.

7

Being Responsive to the Customer

. . . the world is filled with the kind of customers who deserve the care and attention I advocate, and I'd be willing to jump through hoops to win and keep them.

If you had the idea, before getting into this book, that IBM became great because it had vast resources or a product that couldn't be duplicated by others, you must realize by now that IBM's greatness has been built on some very simple ideas and principles. Nothing very complicated or profound — little things that, I hope, are still being taught to children by their parents, teachers and religious leaders. Things like thoughtfulness, courtesy and integrity.

No magic formula or guarded secret keeps customers 'married' to IBM long after their equipment is installed and their check deposited. It's just that IBM approaches the customer, *after* the sale, with the same interest and attention as when he was the prospect to be courted.

IBMers are not Pollyannas or altruists; they're pragmatists — realists who know which side their bread is buttered on. They know they'll be out of work if there are no customers. They also know that although their ambitions may be boundless, there's a limit to the number of customers they can acquire. So while they work very hard to get a new customer, they work even harder to hold on to the ones they have. Someone once said I behaved as if every IBM customer were on the verge of leaving, and that I'd do anything to keep them from bolting. There's a bit of truth in that. IBM is part of a huge industry, and I've always respected the competition. If they want to garner a larger share of the market, they have to compete head-on with IBM. They have to be innovative and smart – and they're both. That's why I might be caught looking over my shoulder, acting a little paranoid. But there is no truth to the suggestion that I'd have done *anything* to get or hold on to a customer. I would never do anything that either I or IBM considered improper or unethical.

There are certain places in the world where the mode of doing business includes bribes and kickbacks. Lots of companies go along with this: 'When in Rome, do as the Romans do.' Well, I don't buy this kind of thinking and neither does IBM. I don't understand how you can have one set of principles for the United States and another set for other parts of the world. No, I wouldn't do *anything* to make a sale, and there were times when I'd refuse to sell someone, on a matter of principle. Fortunately, the world is filled with the kind of customers who deserve the care and attention I advocate, and I'd be willing to jump through hoops to win and keep them.

It seems to me that most companies are a lot better at prospecting for new customers and selling those prospects than maintaining their customer list. They are *sales*-driven, putting money into campaigns designed to bring in leads. They can easily measure how successful they are: how many leads the promotion pulled in and how much each lead cost them. Leads are then turned over to their sales force, and again they can easily measure their success and compute the cost. That's OK as far as it goes, but it's not far enough for a *market*-driven organization. Of course, sales is a very important part of marketing – for some businesses it is the most important part – but it's not the whole thing, and I think that too many companies fail to realize this. By separating selling from the marketing function, they often separate the customer from their long-range plans. At IBM, our field people are called marketing reps, not sales reps, for a good reason: They know that their involvement with a customer just begins with closing the sale. It's much more difficult to measure the cost of keeping a customer than to calculate the cost of getting him in the first place. As far as I'm concerned, customer maintenance is imperative to doing business – and can be the difference between a company that struggles to stand still and one that enjoys healthy growth.

Anyone who stops worrying about a customer once he's delivered his goods should mull over the idea of the *inverted organizational structure*. Take your pyramidal organizational chart and upend it: the longer you look at it, the more sense it makes. The traditional structure shows the chief executive officer in the top box; below him are the top-ranking officers, followed by middle management, and at the bottom of the chart are the marketing or sales reps. Below them, implied if not shown, are the customers. Too often, that's where they're relegated by the people who depend on them most – to the bottom of the heap. But once you set that chart on end, with the CEO on the bottom and the customers on top, it illustrates what should be your company's priorities and goals.

In a truly market-driven organization, the customer is considered first and foremost. Of course, everyone loves this concept *as a customer* – at a restaurant, in a department store, buying a car, or whatever. IBM's customers are in that enviable position at the top of the organizational chart. That's why IBM's so tough to beat.

Being Big, Acting Small

There's a tendency today to look back with bittersweet nostalgia at the time when we were a nation of small shopkeepers. Many people are saddened that the mom-and-pop businesses have given way to big chains and large corporations. Expensive research, ever-growing competition and the tremendous cost of doing business made it impossible for many businesses to stay small; to stay small often means to self-destruct. We can't turn back the clock and become again a nation of craftsmen and tradespeople. Even most of those kids of the sixties who abhorred the way our society was headed have given up their communes and their idea that *only* small is beautiful or worthwhile. And those who lament the loudest for the good old days would probably fight to keep their cars and TVs and long-distance telephone calls – none of which could be produced and operated by a simple proprietorship.

What we long for, I think, is the personal touch of the small business person – the grocer who knew our name, the fruit and vegetable peddler who brought his produce to our door. The doctor who made house calls.

Well, I don't think a company has to be small to act small. Even a giant can be gentle and helpful and kind. It's not the size of a corporation or the number of people it employs that alienates customers, making them yearn for the good old days. It takes only one or two insensitive corporate employees to convince a person that he's dealing with an impersonal mono- lithic giant. After all, few people get entangled in a big company's bureaucracy when they make a purchase. How many employees does it take to negotiate a car deal with you? No more than your great-grandfather dealt with when he purchased a handmade carriage from a local craftsman. And there's no doubt in my mind that there were plenty of short-tempered, impatient business people in the good old days. The point is, it's foolish to blame bad manners on big business. If you walk into an IBM Product Center tomorrow to inquire about a personal computer, and a salesperson treats you with respect and willingly spends whatever time is necessary to satisfy your interest, you're going to feel good about the experience. You're not going to give a hoot if that rep is part of an organization that employs 400,000 people or if he's the proprietor.

It may be more difficult for the folks at IBM to project a personal one-on-one attitude because of the company's size, but they do it. They do it because the customer is considered their number one priority. If IBM can do it, with hundreds of thousands of employ- ees, and tens of thousands of managers, in hundreds of locations spread all over the world, then any company can do it.

There's no way of quantifying how many customers are lost because of little human errors – not returning a phone call, being late for an appointment, failing to say thank you, taking an account for granted. As far as I'm concerned, these 'little' things can be the difference between a very successful company and a failure.

Little Things

If you don't return phone calls promptly or answer your mail quickly, if you break appointments at the last minute, without a darned good reason, or have people sitting on their hands because you're late to appointments you do keep – what kind of message are you sending out? You're saying, 'Hey, customer, you're not really very important to me or my company.' I'll tell you this – I wouldn't want to do business with you. If I'm not sure that you'll return my phone calls, how can I feel sure that you'll expedite my order?

I wonder about the ability of people who don't have the time to answer letters and return phone calls. My job kept me as busy as anyone in our business, but I always found time to respond to customers' letters or phone calls within a day. If I was traveling, an assistant let them know when I'd respond – and I don't think I ever made a liar out of anyone. If I told a customer I would phone him by a certain time, and found that for some reason I couldn't, that customer received a call from my office. If I discovered that I'd be late for an appointment – even a few minutes late – whoever expected me was notified. I respected my customers' time just as I respected my own.

I wrote a lot of notes. Whenever I visited a customer or one visited me, I wrote to thank him for the time he spent with me, and to review whatever we discussed.

If I was his guest for lunch or he was mine, I dropped him a thank-you note. None of these people were taken for granted. You have to let customers know how important they are. Every time a customer is lost, you weaken the sales base; the longer you keep a customer, the greater the equity in the marketing investment.

Too many companies start off on the wrong foot with a new customer by mishandling the initial order. Errors in setting up the account, which lead to wrong billings; a foul-up by the credit department, which delays the order and perhaps embarrasses the customer; improper handling of the paperwork by the shipping department – all errors that could have been avoided with a little care – can negate the good work the salesperson did to bring in the new account. Errors can be corrected, of course, but they're held against you and keep you scrambling. Life is easier when you do things right the first time. Casey Stengel said: 'When you hit a home run you can take your time running the bases.'

From the customer's point of view, nothing could be more frustrating than a continual battle with a supplier's billing department. Hours can be wasted in trying to untangle the mess one or two sloppy entries can cause. IBM makes mistakes too, and some of them could have been avoided. But it makes a continual conscious effort to eliminate them. By that, I mean that IBM doesn't simply wait for an error to occur and then quickly react – although I can assure you that it does quickly react. But it also tries to study the areas where little frustrating mistakes are likely to happen and nip them in the bud.

I've advised marketing reps to introduce new customers to the accounts receivable person – in person. In my opinion, nothing beats having internal people interface with the customers they serve. And it's good to get out of the office and meet the customers on their turf. It's important for people who have to deal with one another on money matters to develop a personal relationship. People should have a better understanding of an account than they can get from credit applications and cold numbers. At times, it can be more difficult when it comes to asking for money; because the relationship is more personal, it must be done with more care and sensitivity – but from my point of view, that's good. Some companies think that when it comes to asking for money, the less personal the relationship, the better. And their dun letters reflect their attitude. They're cold and curt and single-minded, and too often they offend the customer. And frequently they're off base. I completely disagree with this approach, and believe that it wastes a golden opportunity to strengthen a relationship with a customer. I don't ever want to lose a customer because of a billing mixup, or because we can't go after owed money with sensitivity.

A customer's ego, like anyone's, needs massaging at times. I don't believe in complimenting someone insincerely, but there are plenty of opportunities for honest flattery or attention. Years ago, I was called in on a highly competitive situation by a West Coast rep. We were trying to convince the management of a large aerospace company to let us handle certain applications that were being processed on a competitor's system. About twenty of our people were working with them, but the decisionmaker was obviously pleased that someone at my level in the company had come to participate. In fact, he said so. Frankly, I was flattered that he was flattered, and I said, 'Look, if we put this deal together, I'll visit you once a month. You and I will sit down together and review how we're doing in meeting the specific installation target dates. This includes the application programming, people training, systems delivery dates, and all aspects of our joint effort.' We got the business. I don't know what my commitment to those monthly meetings contributed to getting the order, but it may have been very important, even critical. The point is, you must use all your resources if you want to win a customer. You have to be sensitive to customers' needs, and sometimes those needs include a factor that is not product-connected. Incidentally, I kept my promise and, in time, established a wonderful relationship for IBM and for me personally. Of course, I couldn't make the same promise to every customer – it's a matter of putting one's time to the best possible use.

I called on many customers while I was in IBM management. I always followed up the visit with a letter, thanking them for their time and their business, and summarizing our discussion and whatever plans we made. Then, at the appropriate time, depending on the situation, I phoned to be sure that the customer was satisfied with the results.

It takes time and energy and a good tickler system to build a solid relationship with a customer, but it's important. And if anyone says that what I'm describing is busy work, I say that person doesn't understand marketing.

In all my years with IBM, I never considered the amount of business involved when it came to solving

171

a customer's problem. When I was corporate vice-president of marketing, a complaint addressed only to 'The Marketing Manager' was forwarded to me. An elderly man who had one of our first typewriter models was upset because his order for three black typewriter ribbons was shipped in the wrong color. He said that he had been trying to straighten out this problem but received no satisfaction. I wrote immediately, expressing my regret that we had inconvenienced him and assuring him that his order would be expedited promptly and properly. A few days later, I phoned to make sure that he had received the ribbons. And you can be sure that I investigated to find out why the error occurred. This was no grandstand play. Little problems can be symptomatic of big problems – and the time to solve them is when you hear about them.

It's essential to convey to every customer that you value his business, regardless of size. The bigger your organization is, the more important it is for you to relay this message. You never want your small customers to perceive that they're being treated indifferently, or differently from your big customers. I've been told, 'If I don't give you my business you're not going to worry about it, because IBM has thousands of customers that are more important than my company.' Nothing is further from the truth. The combined impact of IBM's small customers on annual sales volume is tremendous. It's the composite of these individual customers that formed the foundation of the company, and it has grown and prospered as a result of their support. When it comes to any policy or marketing decisions, IBM considers the small customer, just as it considers the big one. I've heard people say, 'In our business, 80 percent of our income comes from 20 percent of our customer list, so our policies are designed to keep the 20 percent happy. The rest have to look out for themselves.' In the long run, that kind of attitude will be destructive, and it's one I cannot accept. As a matter of fact, I've always been so sensitive about a small customer's perceiving a slight that I've doubled my effots to prove him wrong.

Brilliant ideas or an expensive PR campaign aren't necessary to improve the way a company is perceived by its customers. It can usually be done by attending to the little details. It's an important part of taking care of business. After I addressed an industry conference recently, someone said: 'There's a lot of talk about excellence in business today, Buck. What does it mean to you?' I answered with the first thought that popped into my mind: 'Excellence means doing the little things well – doing a thousand things one percent better rather than doing one thing a thousand percent better. It's demonstrating to your customer and peers that you're willing to give extra effort, and take an extra step to assure a good job.' It all gets back to value-added selling. You simply can't neglect the little things and be successful.

The Occasional Sacrifice

When I told you that I wasn't a workaholic, I meant it. My private time is very important to me, but every so often a business situation comes up that dips into the hours I usually set aside for myself and my family. I never resent putting in that extra time, especially when it benefits a customer. It's an investment that always pays off.

From the beginning of my IBM career, I realized that an excellent performance required that my customers be happy with what I did. When I was a neophyte marketing rep, I sold a computer system to a wire spring company in Cleveland. It was my biggest sale at the time, and I wanted them to be as pleased and excited as I was. They had a difficult payroll problem, and were worried about the time it would take to transfer everything from a manual system on to punch cards and then into the computer. I spoke with our systems engineers and we agreed to do something special for this new customer. We worked through the weekend — forty-eight hours straight — and when the company opened for business Monday morning, the system was in place and the payroll ready to be processed. The customer was elated and grateful, and I had the satisfaction of knowing that the systems engineers and I had done an excellent job. It was a rewarding experience, especially so early in my career. I liked the good feeling and was happy to repeat it whenever it was necessary.

No one should be expected to operate in overdrive continuously, but there are times when an extra effort and a small sacrifice can be very important to you and your customer. If repeat business is as important to you as it is to IBM, you must be committed to the extra effort. A seductive advertising campaign and a price with most of the profit squeezed out of it are not enough. It's one thing to get the initial order, but quite another to have the customer stay with you year after year.

During my tenure as head of marketing, IBM grew from a $10 billion company to a $50 billion company, and we didn't do it by selling price. Most customers are not looking for the cheapest solutions to their problems. They expect to pay a fair price for what they buy. And what they are buying from companies like IBM is usually a real solution to a problem – not a quick fix. The quality of the equipment they invest in is certainly important to them, but even more important is the quality of the people whom they must depend on to service it. *They're buying peace of mind and a good night's sleep*. Customers perceive IBM as a company they can count on in a crisis. There's no doubt in my mind that IBM has earned that perception not because it tries to project a caring image in its advertisements – but because it is willing to make an extra effort and an occasional sacrifice to help a customer. Any customer.

Here's an interesting 'case'. After Irv Levey acquired this book for Harper & Row, he noticed that almost every business machine in the publisher's New York headquarters was an IBM. He asked Bill Baker, the company's comptroller, 'How come? Are they cheaper? Are they superior? Why IBM?' They're not cheaper; Bill Baker was sure of that. And he couldn't swear that they were absolutely the best machines available. But one thing Baker was sure of: IBM's service organization was the best in the world. They were totally dependable and, at times, did incredible things for their customers. Then he told Irv about a time when the company's main computer, in Scranton, Pennsylvania, went down because a very inexpensive small part malfunctioned. It was very unusual for this part to cause a problem, and there was no replacement for it anywhere in the area. However, IBM quickly located one in Colorado, sent a jet to pick it up, and had the computer in full operation within twenty-four hours of the mishap. It took an extra effort by IBM to keep this customer happy. It paid off many times over. And although the incident took place years ago, before Bill Baker became a top executive at Harper's, it was one of the first things that popped into his mind when he was asked, 'Why IBM?'

Avoiding End Zone Saves

No football coach wants to see his team put in a position where the quarterback is forced to pass on the last play of the game. It's especially frustrating if he has the win in his pocket and fumbles it away. Desperation plays cause ulcers. At IBM, everything possible is done to avoid having to make desperate moves to keep an account on the books. It's tough enough when you lose an initial order in a competitive situation, but it's really rough when you're losing a customer you had previously won. The situation becomes intolerable when it's happening because of customer neglect. To me, neglecting an established account is as great a marketing sin as not following up on a bona fide lead.

A company that keeps in touch with its customers is rarely surprised by the kind of problem that loses accounts. To avoid having to make 'end zone saves', you must build into your marketing program a way of keeping in touch with your customer *even when you have nothing to sell*. You never want to be in the position of hearing a distraught customer say: 'Where were you when this problem was developing? You're the experts – you would have spotted it had you been here. Why are you showing up now that we put one of your competitors on the case?'

As far as I'm concerned, the most effective contact you have with a *satisfied* customer is that contact between sales – even if you don't know when the next sale might be made. Many sales organizations disagree completely with me on this. They say that an account with no immediate need for their product is off limits to the rep. Once you sold them, stay away – why look for trouble? Besides, it's too expensive to call on an account unnecessarily. Such organizations are short-sighted. They can't see beyond today's call report.

I wanted our people to find a good reason to call on the satisfied account, even if it took some creative thinking. They can check out the system, making sure there are no minor problems; they might drop off an interesting article that appeared in a trade journal not readily available to the customer, or pass on information regarding an industry meeting. Whatever. Becoming used to seeing the rep – and not only when he's trying to sell – the customer should think: 'This guy really does have my interest at heart. He's accessible. If I have a problem, I'll go to him first.'

When companies, or reps, develop this kind of relationship with a customer, the odds are that they'll never find themselves trapped into making desperation moves to keep the relationship going.

The Program of Reconciliation

Although IBM does everything a company can do to prevent the loss of a customer, occasionally one is lost. Let's face it, IBM's marketing organization is tens of thousands of individuals who have minds and wills of their own and are at various levels of development so far as their business skills are concerned. The company does a marvelous job of recruiting and training, but it's not perfect. Well, whatever the reason for losing an account, IBM doesn't take the loss lightly. It wants that customer back. Once it knows for certain that a customer has a firm commitment with a competitor, IBM steps aside until the competitor has had an opportunity to install his equipment on that specific application. There's no legal reason for this – but IBM thinks it's a tasteful way of doing business, and has made it a matter of policy. It's the same kind of thinking that's behind the company's policy never to knock a competitor. However, it doesn't make IBM any less intense or committed to getting the customer back.

The first step in the reconciliation, as with any other failed relationship, is to find out what went wrong. It might be a misunderstanding between the customer and an IBM service organization. It might be a personality conflict between the customer's contact and the rep. It could be a political problem in the customer's house – a new authority wanting to make his presence felt. Or maybe the competitor's rep did a terrific job of convincing the customer that he could deliver a superior product.

Once the cause of the failure is understood, a solution is sought. It could be a new approach, a redesigned program, a change in equipment or a shift in personnel.

IBM people are patient but persistent. Just as they never take their customers for granted, neither should the competitors. Sometimes it requires a year or more to win back a lost account, but IBM's average in recouping lost business is quite high.

Why is losing a customer so challenging? For one

thing, a lost customer has an immediate impact on sales volume. The company invests a lot to get the customer in the first place. It counts on repeat business, equity in the existing customer list. Turning over inventory is exciting – turning over a customer list is frightening. When you lose an account, you risk a snowball effect. A dissatisfied customer may complain to ten others and influence them negatively. The competitor who won the customer from you might broadcast his victory to all who will listen. That can't help your image and can have a demoralizing effect on the rep in the field. And you don't increase your sales base by replacing a lost customer. Every time you lose a customer, you have to sell another one just to stand still.

True Partnerships

It's easier to keep an account than it is to regain one. Easier, that is, if your orientation is long-term relationships. And the basis for an enduring association is, of course, understanding and concern. A company that views a business relationship strictly from a selfish vantage point has no right to expect loyalty from the other principal. I don't see how you can be successful, in the long run, if the customer isn't strengthened by his involvement with you. I honestly believe that any good that is done for the customer is good for you. And the flip side of that is just as true. If you hurt the customer, you hurt yourself. That's why IBM wants its field people to represent the customer with as much zeal as they devote to IBM. I assure you that there is no conflict of interest when it's done properly.

179

A team of IBMers asked me to help them with a customer that was one of the nation's largest banks. It was a tough competitive situation. Another computer company had made a strong pitch for the business, and as the meeting, at the bank's headquarters, progressed, it became evident that the executives were leaning toward the other company. The bank's president was very impressed with the technological aspects of the competitor's presentation. He was obviously caught up in the bits and bytes, and I would have antagonized him had I debated their relative value.

I listened very attentively as he had his say, and when he was finished I responded. 'I have only one thing to ask, and nothing more,' I said. 'Do you want to do business with a hardware vendor or do you want a partner?'

There was nothing tricky or clever about the question. It was honest. I truly believed that we had something very special to offer this account, something that went far beyond the technology of our machines – our sincere interest in their well-being.

'I want a partner,' he said, after considering the question for a few moments. Then he walked over to me, extended his hand and said, 'Buck, shake hands with your new partner.'

I always wanted every customer to feel a partnership relationship with IBM. Like friendship, marriage or a legal partnership, the kind of relationship I advocate requires a greater commitment, and acceptance of more responsibility, than any ordinary buyer-seller relationship. The seller should never do anything that is self-serving, anything for short-term gain, anything that might jeopardize a long-term relationship. It's a very nice way of doing business. It casts both parties in roles that are far removed from those of adversaries, each trying to squeeze the 'best deal' out of the other.

The highest-profile IBM 'partnerships' are those with the national accounts. General Motors is an example. A team of IBMers, headed by an account executive, works full-time with GM. IBM has offices at their headquarters and manpower located at each of their many divisions. It's not unusual for a marketing rep to report daily to one such account, where he spends 90 percent of his time.

Customers sometimes confuse the IBM staff with theirs. It was always music to my ears when they said, 'I forget who's on my payroll and who's on yours.'

When you work that closely with a customer, you know that you have reached the highest level of customer-partner satisfaction.

A lot of salespeople make a go of it by taking the path of least resistance. 'Give 'em what they want, and let them worry about it if they make a mistake' is a common attitude. That doesn't work if you believe in partnership selling. I've been in competitive selling situations where the customer wanted a smaller, less expensive installation than I *knew* he needed. I could not sell him what he wanted, without feeling that I wasn't benefiting him. Not if I had done my homework. Not if I had spent days on his shop floor studying his operation, interviewing his foremen, engineers and production people. It's exactly the same if I concluded that what the customer wanted was more equipment than he needed. When I tried to increase or decrease a client's order, it was because I *knew* I was right. It's a matter of integrity. There's a time when you have to take a stand, even if it means losing the order. Of course, taking such a stand wouldn't make sense in all selling situations. If a customer wanted ten typewriters and I thought he needed twelve, I wasn't going to walk away from the order. No harm done, and when he found out I was right, he'd order more. But I'd have to take a stand in a case where I was selling a complex installation that might require equipment modifications and a custom-designed program. An error by the customer could cost him a great deal in terms of future work disruption and investment.

Sticking to your guns may not be the easiest way to get the initial order, but it pays off in the long run.

In our business, sometimes a customer outgrows his system more quickly than he or we expected. Forecasting future needs is hardly an exact science, so at IBM an attempt is made to document every assumption that went into the decision to install a particular product. It's good to have that documentation in those instances when, a year or two after a sale is made, the customer comes in anguish and says, 'How did this happen? I can't handle these increases in volume. How could such a mistake have been made?' Of course, the company's assumptions are rooted in the forecasts made by the customer. So long as there are records of those expectations, IBM can demonstrate that the decision at the time was right. The purpose is not to hide behind those numbers but to help the customer understand IBM's response to them.

The quality of the company's relationship to its customers is affected by its morality and expertise. Although it's said that you can't legislate morality, when it comes to the way IBM's people relate to its customers, IBM tries. And its people are expected to become experts in whatever marketplace they are asked to service. It's IBM's way of making sure that the company's response to any customer's inquiry or problem will be authoritative, intelligent and fair.

Although the teams it sends into the field are highly trained in their area of expertise, IBM still goes to outside sources for reinforcement — consulting firms and universities, for example. It goes to the outside on a regularly scheduled basis, as well as ad hoc. Each year, for example, a group of Harvard MBAs is invited to study a particular problem. The point of this is to maintain a certain balance in IBM's interpretation of customers' needs. Many professors with outstanding expertise in business and industry are available for consultation. It surprises me that more companies — especially small firms — don't take advantage of this rich source of knowledge.

The major manufacturers and packagers of consumer products do a tremendous job of collecting data to better understand their customers. Their market researchers, through in-depth surveys and diligent probing, have learned that the average American puts 3.2 ice cubes in his soft-drink glass; blows his nose 256 times a year; writes 24 checks a month; consumes 95 hot dogs, 283 eggs, 5 pounds of yogurt, 9 pounds of cereal and 2 pounds of peanut butter per year. Incredible! They even know that 47 percent of us put water on our brush before we apply the toothpaste and 15 percent water the brush after the toothpaste is applied. I've never been a trivia game player, but this is fascinating stuff. But what's really impressive is the depth of the inquiry. The companies that sponsor this type of consumer survey are in the most competitive of businesses. They have to know their customers so well that they can anticipate and respond to their questions, concerns and worries. Most businesses don't have to think in terms of their average customer, nor do they need to deal with consensus opinions. They can communicate directly with their customers, and uncover their needs and concerns. And respond in a thoughtful, courteous, honest way – if they appreciate the importance of holding on to a customer, and are smart enough to do it. You don't have to be a genius.

8

Service, Service, Service . . . and More Service

While everybody wants it, most don't want to give it.

Service is a tremendous source of revenue for IBM. In fact, if the revenue generated by IBM's domestic service alone went into a separate corporation, that company would rank within the top 100 companies of 1985 in the *Fortune* 500 listing.

IBM pioneered the idea that *selling* and *servicing* were inseparable parts of the marketing function. And although *Roget's Thesaurus* doesn't consider the two words to be synonyms, IBM does. Seventy-plus years ago, when Tom Watson, Sr, proclaimed service to be the backbone of sales, selling was almost entirely a battle of wits: a contest between the buyer, who had some money in his pocket, and the seller, who wanted it.

Selling in general has changed since those days. The contest between buyer and seller is more subtle; more civilized. Today's salespeople study the art of persuasion, and take courses in negotiating. Too often they concentrate on buzzwords, angles and hooks, rather than quality and service.

Psychologists are paid to come up with clues to a prospect's vulnerability, then wordsmiths and media specialists zap him with messages that make products irresistible.

Today, some products are hyped in a way that purposely ignores quality. Yes, selling has changed since 1914, when Watson, Sr, began implementing his notion about the art. It seems to me, however, that the changes aren't really fundamental. They are mostly changes in style, format and technology.

I sold service during my entire professional life. I bought IBM's line not because it was glib or slick but because service worked for me. It made me a topnotch salesperson.

Why haven't more companies recognized the fact that the most reliable contributor to building a solid sales base is giving the customer the best possible service?

Modern business has certainly focused its attention on convenience. You don't have to go far to spend your money today. It seems that you can buy just about anything without leaving your home. Merely dial 1–800 and have your credit card number ready.

Of course, I'm not putting down convenience. IBM has its 800 numbers too. But convenience is not enough, and sometimes it's a misnomer. Buying a product without leaving one's easy chair may seem convenient until the product arrives in a thousand pieces, with instructions that are loosely translated from the Japanese. What happens when one of the parts is missing and the 800 number is connected to an answering machine hundreds of miles away?

When business turned its attention to new channels of distribution, it certainly made an important impact on our buying habits, and our expectations. In many ways it's been a bonanza for lots of businesses. However, companies like IBM, which have enthusiastically committed themselves to giving the best possible service to their customers, have also experienced prosperity, *plus* the security of an ever-growing customer base.

The general attitude about service is an interesting paradox. While everybody wants it, most don't want to give it. Some individuals may consider giving service to be a downer – a throwback to the days of the obsequious servant. But I'll tell you this – I doubt if any of IBM's thousands of service people feel demeaned by what they do for a living. More about that in a moment, but what about businesses that struggle against a difficult economy, foreign competition and an unending stream of new products that vie for the customer's allegiance? Why don't these companies understand the importance of service? I think it's partly because they can't quantify its value, especially after they've made the sale. They consider the costs involved to be nonrecuperated expenses. To me, it doesn't matter how you account for the cost of servicing a customer; the important thing, in the long run, is to consider it an investment in the future.

I'm concerned here about the service that takes place *after* the sale is made. Some businesses, of course, have no contact at all with a customer once the goods and money change hands. Having one product to sell per customer, with little or no chance of repeat business, they are totally sales-driven. But too many firms that *do* depend on repeat business to keep afloat seem to forget the customer once they land him. At least, they behave that way.

IBM can't forget the importance of its old customers or its commitment to give them the best service possible. It is part of IBM's creed, and it's reaffirmed every working day by everyone in the company.

When it comes to service, IBM may have written the book. It took more than a simple commitment to reach the company's present level of excellence – it took a major investment in time, research, manpower and money. And the work and investment are ongoing. It's worth it. When IBM tells a customer that a product it buys from the company is only the tip of the iceberg, IBM means it. A marketing rep may sell a machine or an application, but what he delivers is the concern and expertise of a tremendously talented and committed staff. Included are administrative people, technical specialists, systems engineers, service representatives and managers who work in every capacity throughout the company. The service provided goes far beyond making certain that the product sold delivers what was promised. IBM people share their market research, and what they know about advertising and even accounting. They invite customers to IBM-sponsored industry seminars and conferences, providing an environment where customers learn not only from IBM but from each other.

The size of a customer's purchase is not a factor in determining what IBM provides in service. The in-depth service described above is available to every customer.

IBM decided years ago that to be the most successful company in the world, it must have an exciting, flexible, sensitive service program to maintain old customers, create new ones and make people want to do business with IBM. A good service program would not be satisfactory. It had to be better than that. When IBM's commitment to being the best service organiz-ation in the world, bar none, regardless of industry, was announced to employees, the spirit within the company soared. An IBM culture was created, which started with recruits in their basic training program. That spirit would prevail throughout their entire careers. Everyone was sharing the same commitment – to provide an overwhelming level of service, une-qualled by anyone, and to achieve the highest level of customer satisfaction.

Think of the pride of the salesperson who can tell a customer: 'If you incorporate my ideas and products into your operation, we will never let you down. Servicing your company will be our top priority.' He can say it without fear because his organization will not let him down.

IBM doesn't want to lose a customer, ever. It tries to give superior day-to-day service so that customers wouldn't even consider doing business with anyone else. But one is lost occasionally, and when it happens it stings IBMers' pride. They never blame it on the customer. They want to know what went wrong, and when they find out, they take steps to prevent a recurrence.

Any company can strengthen its position with cur-rent customers by improving its service program. It probably wouldn't take additional real estate or a big investment in equipment or personnel. What it takes is a major commitment of the company's top manage-ment, and the resolution that, in time, every employee must make the same commitment.

Building Service into the Product

Service can't be an afterthought. It must be an important part of the marketing plan, and a serious consideration throughout the development of the product, from its very inception. A new product should never be introduced before service has been thought out and tested.

At IBM, service people live at the development site of a new product. They design the maintenance techniques and deal with such questions as: What training will be required to service the product? What diagnostics can be built into it? What is the appropriate support delivery system? Where should spare parts be stocked? In what quantities?

An interlock process during the initial planning integrates engineering, manufacturing, marketing *and servicing*. For a product to get a development go-ahead, each of the four functions is required to verify that it has the skills and resources to do its part.

Of course, it's a lot easier for an engineer to design a product if he doesn't have to worry about its maintenance; and if he doesn't look down the road, it may seem cheaper. But it isn't. I've heard of companies that quickly designed a product, then rushed it into the marketplace without any consideration for its maintenance. Soon they discovered that the cost of servicing it was prohibitive, and the entire project was scrapped. It's almost impossible for anyone with an IBM orientation to fathom this, but I know it happens.

IBM's engineers know that a product's design must be practical and economical. A product mustn't be overdesigned or underdesigned if it's to be serviced with minimal difficulties. And as the product is being developed, the company must be kept apprised of the servicing problems that are foreseen. Important servicing questions must be resolved by the time the product is ready for the market. Are the skills needed for servicing already in the house and available when needed? Must some of the service reps be retrained or do additional people have to be hired? Is there a shortage of the kind of skilled service people needed for this new product? If there is a shortage, is it so acute that it's necessary to build redundancy into the product to reduce the need for specific service?

Just as cost-effective redundancy is built into a design of a product to reduce the possibility of a customer's equipment going down, a program of preventive maintenance is put into motion right from the point of sale. Service schedules are established for every product IBM produces, including typewriters, copiers, terminals, and small and large computers. Service reps make regular calls and inspect the equipment. Sometimes the call is for a specific maintenance procedure, or because a certain component may have developed a troublesome history and the service person wants to shortstop a potential headache. Sometimes the call is for a general checkup. The rep isn't looking for trouble; he's just testing to make sure there isn't any.

IBM people don't want to interrupt the customer's operation, so when trouble does develop, they do everything possible to eliminate the down time entirely or at least limit it to the barest minimum. If a service rep identifies the problem as being in hardware, he replaces the faulty element with a new one. Not only is this the quickest way to get the equipment running; it's also the most economical.

The important thing is to have the service people work hand in hand with the technical people. When IBM built a new typewriter in Lexington, Kentucky, hundreds of service reps worked on the manufacturing line. It was essential that they have firsthand knowledge of how the product was made. After all, they were the ones who would be sent into the field to service it. They had a complete understanding of the machines, and were able to foresee the type of servicing problems that might occur, so they argued that additional redundancy be built into units. Because they did, the service time needed for these typewriters was greatly reduced.

Often, to enhance its *ease of use*, a product is brought into an IBM test center. Here, nonprofessionals read the product's promotional materials, study the application code and operate the new machines. They do this while being observed by engineers and 'human factor' people. What is learned has a marked effect on the finished product.

At times, the service people request that a particular product be introduced on a stage basis, with testing in perhaps eight major cities to study the product's service needs before it is distributed nationally.

In a sense, IBM reinvents service every time it creates a new product.

The Difference-Makers

Service rep – the IBMer who actually services a customer's equipment – is a job classification that carries great responsibility and respect. (As noted, 'service person' in IBM parlance is far from the proverbial guy in rumpled coveralls with grease under his fingernails. IBM service reps come to work dressed in the same fashion as a marketing rep or an executive. And why not? They're very important business people and IBM wants its customers to sense immediately that they are dealing with a very special breed of service person.)

To IBM's more than 25,000 field service people, *the customer comes first, absolutely*. They know that the equipment IBM installs is vital to the operation of a company. If it goes down, a whole plant can go down. This is especially true in a catalytic operation such as a petrochemical company, where the entry of its gasoline and crude oil is based upon a process control system, and if one computer system fails, the plant grinds to a halt. And it's true of manufacturers that rely to a great extent on robots, or any business whose inventory is computer-controlled. Customers depend on the service reps to keep their operation running smoothly twenty-four hours a day.

A service rep can be either a generalist who services a variety of machines (typewriters, copiers, word processors, small computers) or a specialist in, say, large computers. In either case, he is thoroughly trained before he's put in a customer environment. The service division has a strict rule never to allow anyone to service a product he isn't completely familiar with, even if it's closely related to a piece he has mastered. While there might be little doubt that he could service it, the company won't relax the rule and risk an error.

As is true with every IBMer who works in this field, the service rep's performance is enhanced when he understands the meaning of being on a team, and takes advantage of the company's available resources to do the job at hand. He must learn which resources to tap and where to go to get the information to satisfy the customer. He depends on *teamwork*.

Besides the mechanical and technical training they receive, service reps go through IBM's basic orientation and educational program along with the marketing reps and the systems engineers.

For the past few years, a *Fortune* magazine survey has proclaimed IBM to be the most admired company in America. It's an honor that everyone at IBM is proud of and rightfully shares in, but if there's any single facet of IBM's operation that has 'the best' written all over it, it's service. Creeds, policies and programs document the company's desire to serve, which may even border on compulsion; but it really comes down to the people, to this army of good citizens, dressed in their business suits, proudly representing IBM and willingly helping every customer. It's a matter of pride and integrity to them and to the company.

The way people view IBM is fascinating to me. What they're really impressed with, I think, is the adherence to common courtesy and old-fashioned values. It seems a little strange, considering the fact that so many business people ignore those values in their own business relationships. Their indifference bothers me. I call it 'psychosclerosis': a hardening of the attitudes. Their heads are filled with thoughts like: 'It's someone else's problem, not mine.' 'Why should I get involved?' 'If I'm off the hook contractually, the heck with them.' If your attitude is one of apathy and avoidance, you can't expect those who represent you to be any different.

Calendar Integrity

I can't tolerate bad manners or sloppy work. I always expected the people I worked with to be considerate to me, to their co-workers and, of course, to our customers. I'm a nut on what I call calendar integrity. I want meetings to start on time, and I want everyone who's supposed to participate to be there. I want my phone calls returned and my memos answered and deliveries made when promised. People who can't do those things have no business in a sales-oriented, customer-driven company. Personally, I don't know what business they do belong in.

A company can't give good service — not what I consider good service — unless its people are committed to calendar integrity. Everyone who ever worked for me knows exactly what that term means to me. They know that when they have an appointment with me and are late — even a few minutes late — I don't let it slide by. It's not the few minutes that matters; it's the lack of respect for someone else's time. I come down hard on those who do not perform the simple courtesies and tasks, and I'm consistent.

Once, I had an appointment with the president of a multibillion-dollar manufacturing company near Chicago. I flew in from New York and, with a group of IBMers, went to his office for a 10 A.M. meeting. We were right on time, but were ushered into a reception area by a secretary, and waited half an hour. Finally, I said to the people with me, 'We've waited long enough. Let's go.'

They felt somewhat uneasy about leaving. 'But, Buck, we have to work with these people on a day-to-day basis.'

195

'That's baloney,' I told them. 'There's no reason for anyone from our company to be treated this way.' And we left.

The manufacturer's president called me that afternoon at the local IBM office and said, 'Hey, Buck, I thought we had an appointment set up for this morning.'

'A ten o'clock appointment,' I said, 'and I was there.'

He immediately rescheduled the meeting, and I guarantee you it started exactly on time. And it was a good one. Calendar integrity must be practiced across the board. I live by it, and I expect others to do the same.

Good values and good business are not contradictory. IBM isn't the only company in the world that's proved that. But I'd like to see the day when the nice things a company does are not viewed as modern business anomalies.

Giving good service is doing a lot of little things right the first time. It starts with each individual taking care of business, hour by hour, day by day. It's the water-drop principle: Each little act, no matter how insignificant it appears, is tremendously important.

The Closer the Better

One of IBM's real strengths is the local support available to the customer. Typically, sales and service people are located in the same building, while strong emphasis is placed on day-to-day dialogue between the two groups. It's vital that they work as a team and understand and respect each other's problems and expertise. The close relationship makes it possible for the reps to sell IBM's service without hesitation. They know that what they promise will be delivered and they're grateful for that. On the other hand, the service people know that their success is directly tied into the new business generated by the salespeople. This kind of interdependency could cause stress and friction between the two groups, but it doesn't – the relationship is warm, friendly and harmonious. Throughout the organization there's a continual meshing of sales, service and education, which is brought as close to the customer as possible. For example, located at most of IBM's regional offices are small groups of specialists called Application Transfer Teams. They focus on leading edge applications; learn every justification, and then help the reps sell it to specific customers. Equally important, they participate in the installation of these applications from one customer to another. Their function is primarily one of passing on outstanding new applications. But, as with many things IBM does, the effort reaps its eventual rewards. The most satisfied customers are those who get the maximum benefit from their investments. If Application Transfer Teams can come up with more uses for the equipment than the customer bargained for, it's a bonus the customer won't forget.

Along the same line, there are Application Marketing Centers across the country where seminars, product demonstrations and business systems planning programs are conducted. There, IBM specialists train customers to maximize the use of their equipment by accessing decisionmaking data within their own organization.

Some of these centers concentrate on the needs of

the retailer; a customer can come to learn about optical scanning systems, for example. Other centers focus on office systems, and there a customer might spend several days learning how the flow of office information can be mechanized.

When You Can't Get as Close as You'd Like

Sometimes a customer needs information, or has an equipment problem, and it's not feasible for him to get to one of the IBM centers, nor for the company immediately to dispatch a service person to his facility. Happily, IBM has developed incredibly successful remote service systems. A customer with an equipment problem can make a toll-free call to an IBM Support Center and describe his problem to one of the technicians there. This expertly trained technician quickly taps into a central data base to search for any similar or identical problems that occurred elsewhere with the same type of equipment. He then finds out how they were diagnosed and corrected. Actually, all IBMers have access to a worldwide network of data banks that contain up-to-the-minute solutions to every kind of equipment or systems problem imaginable.

Via telecommunications, engineers and service people in Poughkeepsie can see exactly what's happening with a machine on the customer's premises in San Francisco, and solve its problem without leaving the IBM facilities. If repairs are required, the necessary service people are sent to do the work.

It's also possible to forecast and prevent an equipment problem by on-line diagnostics. A terminal can be linked to a mainline computer, and then, by using a mathematical model, technicians can locate an impending problem, and correct it before it happens!

Also adding to service productivity are more effective measuring tools. There is, for example, a portable device that plugs into an ailing machine and does everything but take its temperature. This helps to analyze difficult technical problems, saving a tremendous number of man-hours.

Another remote service is performed by connecting a customer's computer with one at the company, which is programmed to analyze the problem.

Here's a statistic that might surprise you: *About 85 percent of the called-in problems are solved immediately on the telephone!* By now it won't surprise you that the company tries to respond to all problems within twenty-four hours.

IBM products need immediate service when there's trouble. It can be catastrophic if a system containing the guts of a business goes down. The closer the customer, the easier the problems are to deal with. But whether next door or halfway around the world from the problem, IBM has the same sense of responsibility.

The Image-Builders

When IBM says it wants its customers to sleep well at night, that it can be counted on to keep their equipment operating, it's completely serious. IBM's reputation for being perhaps the most service-oriented company in the world isn't the result of a successful advertising campaign or PR hype. It's a reputation that came about through years of consistent hard work, and occasionally some downright heroics by service people. Here are a few legendary episodes:

A service rep based in Phoenix was driving to Tempe to deliver a small part a customer needed to restore a malfunctioning data center. But what was usually a short, pleasant drive turned into a nightmare. Torrential rain transformed the Salt River into rampaging rapids, which closed all but two of the sixteen bridges that crossed over to Tempe, causing a bumper-to-bumper traffic jam that changed the normal twenty-five-minute drive to a four-hour crawl. Determined not to lose the entire afternoon to the traffic, the service rep remembered that she had a pair of roller skates in the trunk of her car. She pulled out of the line of traffic, donned the skates, and skated across the bridge and to the customer's rescue!

I could fill a book with this kind of a story. About a service rep who traveled four hundred miles to make a typewriter repair. About a team of our people who traveled by helicopter to get to a lumber mill in a remote section of Oregon.

And we all remember the New York City blackouts. Wall Street came to a standstill; both the New York and the American stock exchanges were shut down, and banking firms were in turmoil. Everyone in IBM's New York City branch offices worked relentlessly to keep every customer's lost time to an absolute minimum. Finding, transporting and installing needed parts and machines was almost a magic act.

During a twenty-five-hour power failure brought on by a heat wave, with outside temperatures in the mid-nineties and no air conditioning, with no elevators and of course no light, IBM people climbed stairs in some of the tallest buildings in New York (including the

World Trade Center) in order to service customers' machines.

A few years ago, on the day before Thanksgiving, a fire broke out on the fifteenth floor of the Reliance Insurance Company in Philadelphia – the site of its computer room. The IBM field manager was notified at 5 A.M., but wasn't allowed to survey the damage until 8:30 that morning. He discovered that all conduit wires were melted and a lot of machines were damaged – twenty keypunches, ten disk drives, a laser printer, twenty tape drives, five communication systems and eighteen key entry units. Using emergency lighting the first twenty-four hours, teams of IBM service people worked in round-the-clock shifts. By Monday morning, Reliance was fully operational. Because IBM service people worked throughout the three-day holiday, Reliance hardly missed a beat.

Hundreds of incredible customer service stories were reported during the 'great blizzards' of 1977 and 1978 in the American Midwest and Northeast. However, such servicing is an everyday occurrence for the IBM service reps working with the Alyeska Pipeline Service Company. The Trans-Alaska Pipeline moves 1.6 billion barrels of crude oil about eight-hundred miles every day, past a series of ten pump stations, each built specifically for arctic conditions. Each station contains IBM terminals linked to a mainframe computer in Anchorage. Alyeska's state-of-the-art computer tracks the oil as it passes through the line, schedules oil into tankers, handles the payroll and word processing, and enables workers at any pump station to order parts instantly.

The two biggest problems for servicing the pipeline are the harsh weather and the remote locations of the pump stations. It's not uncommon for service reps to be exposed to temperatures of forty degrees below zero. They carry winter survival items in their cars – snow boots, blankets, arctic parkas, heavy mittens, and camp stoves to melt snow for water. Travel by small plane to remote places – taking off and landing on Alaska's barren North Slope – makes these frequent trips anything but joyrides. Sometimes it's a major feat simply to open the frozen door of the aircraft. Because of the infrequent scheduled commercial flights into the areas, an otherwise fifteen-minute service call often takes ten hours or more.

Many customers present truly challenging service problems. But coming up with solutions to those problems is part of what IBMers do for a living. Customers expect it of them, and that's the way they want it.

It's no simple task to service the Norfolk Navy Base, with more than 3,100 ships entering and leaving the port every year, but it has to be done. There are all kinds of servicing problems: getting through the tight security; frequent exposure to the open seas; having to cut a hole into the side of a ship to deliver a machine five decks down, by means of slings and dollies; dealing with the rust caused by a nuclear wash-down drill (the spraying of salt water on board to wash off radiation in the event of a nuclear leak); working in incredibly cramped quarters (one service rep described the repairing of a computer on board a submarine as 'like trying to fix a typewriter in a telephone booth'). IBM sells service. It has to deliver.

Planning for Months, Moving in Hours

Moving for any business is stressful, and it's particularly so when an organization's computer operation must be relocated. When a major customer makes the decision to move, IBM service people have their work cut out for them. When you're dealing with a computer system that is vital to the ongoing operation of a company, it's more than packing, shipping and unpacking. The task is approached with the sensitivity and urgency of a surgical team in an operating room. That may sound overdramatic, until you think of the information and important applications stored in the memory of these machines.

The amount of work and time involved in a move can be tremendous. Twenty-four service reps working around the clock, in teams of eight, put in a total of more than seventeen thousand man-hours to relocate the computer system of the McDonnell Douglas Automation Company when their Saint Louis headquarters moved to a seven-building campus.

It took eighteen months of advance planning to move the Arco (Atlantic Richfield Co.) Oil and Gas Division's data processing operation from Dallas to Plano, Texas, about twenty miles away. An estimated four thousand detailed tasks were identified and tracked, using a computerized management control and scheduling system. The move was planned with minute detail and precision, including the schedule for individual trucks, what each would carry, and what would happen when they arrived at the new location. In order for Arco, as well as its fifteen hundred time-sharing users, to have the maximum use of its system during the operation, the move was spread out over several months' weekends and holidays. As always, everything possible was done to keep disruptions to a minimum. Throughout the move, more than fifty-five agencies continued to use the center, with three thousand terminals supporting their on-line users.

For IBM, with its thousands of customers, relocating is an everyday occurrence, yet no two moves are exactly alike. There's nothing automatic about them. Each requires the service reps' individual attention.

During my thirty-four-year career, I witnessed innumerable situations that, in their uniqueness, required not only conscientious but creative servicing. Organizations like the FBI, the CIA, the World Bank, the US Supreme Court, the Nuclear Regulatory Commission, and the White House presented special problems. But whether government agencies, or special enterprises like the 1984 World's Fair and the 1984 Olympics, or small entrepreneurs are in need, the resourcefulness, flexibility and commitment of IBM's service people stand ready to meet every challenge head-on. I tell you this: knowing that the world's greatest field service organization is making every function in the company run more smoothly makes life easier – especially marketing.

9

Measurement and Compensation

IBM doesn't want its people to get frustrated and restless because it has them reaching for carrots they can't quite grasp.

I've taken great care to let you know how IBM feels about its marketing people, but let's face it, we didn't build one of the world's greatest sales organizations by *just caring* for our people. Being concerned helps, all right, but it doesn't build homes, educate children, or pay for cars, boats or vacations. It doesn't assure anyone of a financially trouble-free retirement. Those things take money. And the kind of marketing people who succeed in IBM are as interested in their personal bottom line as the 'numbers people' are in the corporation's bottom line. IBM wants its people to be concerned not only with their own financial health but with the company's too. They will be if they are treated fairly. Every leader of IBM, since the days of Tom Watson, Sr, has known that fair compensation is an important part of fair treatment.

As you already know, this company puts tremendous effort and resources into selecting, recruiting and training its marketing and systems engineering people. It would be foolish to make such an investment in these young people, then waste their potential by using a compensation package that promises a lot more than it delivers.

IBM doesn't want its people to get frustrated and restless because it has them reaching for carrots they can't quite grasp. It doesn't want them to envy competitors' employees, or to look for greener pastures in other industries.

Some companies actually make an effort to turn over their salespeople frequently. By keeping investment in the marketing staff low and getting rid of people before they build up any equity, these organizations think they profit on the turnover. But that's not IBM's style. A professional marketing organization that's capable of building long-lasting relationships with customers is the goal. And IBM is successful at keeping its marketing force pretty much intact. Less than 5 percent leave voluntarily each year, and that includes quite a number who choose to take early retirement. A few are enticed by lucrative offers from companies just starting out in some phase of the industry who are willing to pay dearly for the IBM expertise. Often it's an offer of some sort of partnership. Very few leave to go to the competition. One important reason people don't leave voluntarily is that the IBM money and benefit package is good.

Coming up with a system of compensation that makes sense for everyone is no simple matter. Of course, the total money package must be fair to the employee and to the company, but *how it's paid* can make a difference in how satisfied the employee is, and how well he or she performs.

At IBM, the compensation strategy has to accomplish several things:

206

1. *It has to provide employees with a sense of security*. IBM wants them to concentrate on making their objectives when they're in the field representing the company. They should not be distracted with basic money worries – that is, money needed to feed, clothe and house their family. Their salary should take care of those things, if they manage their affairs sensibly. I'm not suggesting that all employees are told, 'Submit your personal budget to us, and we'll come up with a guaranteed salary to cover it.' But they do know what they're assured of getting, and can budget accordingly. There is an attitude in some companies that sets up the salesperson to sweat out the very minimum. I don't go along with that.

The security aspect of IBM's compensation is enhanced by the reimbursement of travel and other territory expenses, and a generous package of benefits that is one of the best offered by any company, anywhere. When a person receives a substantial part of his or her income in the form of guaranteed salary, insurance, paid vacations, retirement plans and other benefits, the company has the right to 'manage' that employee in a way that's not possible with one who works on straight commission or free lance. So when it comes to guarantees, there are pluses and minuses for both the employer and the employee.

2. Besides providing security for the employee, *the pay package must include strong incentives and motivation*. Some people are satisfied with the base pay, fringes and expenses. IBM tries not to hire such individuals, but is after sales and marketing people who want more than a fixed salary and expenses, and will respond when given the right opportunity. It's necessary to come up with incentives that not only will

encourage excellent performances and high levels of productivity but will deliver a higher income when the reps succeed. The point is, IBM is willing to pay a premium for excellence and achievement. Therefore, an incentive system that works is crucial to the overall success of the company's entire compensation program.

3. In addition to salary and commission, IBM likes to sweeten the lives of especially deserving employees with *awards and rewards*. They're not always announced in advance, and usually come as a surprise to the recipient. They come in the form of cash, gifts or trips, and are tokens of the company's appreciation of superior performance or a specific accomplishment. Even when spontaneous, they are both objective and subjective gestures.

Money in the Bank

First, about the salary: pay packages are designed so that, on average, about one half of the total income of marketing reps, marketing managers and branch managers is derived from their guarantees, or base pay. There are a number of factors that go into a marketing person's base pay: the position, the employee's length of service, and the quality of the employee's overall performance. These reflect the increasing value of experience, expertise and maturity. Along with the growing value of fringe benefits and the retirement package, it's the employee's equity in the company, the return on his or her investment in time and loyalty.

While an employee's salary and job are secure so

long as he or she performs effectively, no one has tenure at IBM. (For thirty-four years I kept listening for those footsteps; some days they were louder than others.) There's pride in the fact that no one has ever been laid off because of cutbacks in programs, departments, products or budgets; but a person will be discharged, regardless of position or longevity, who violates the company's ethics, or falls down on the job and fails to respond to assistance in correcting his or her performance.

Every person has the right to an annual performance appraisal and a face-to-face discussion about it with his manager. If the manager is doing his job properly throughout the year, there should be no surprises at the annual appraisal meeting. That is, he should be on top of things, and his people should be apprised, on an ongoing basis, of any developing problems or dissatisfaction. This evaluation of an employee's performance helps determine the size of his merit increase. It is possible for an employee to go through a year without receiving an increase in salary, because IBM does not give cost-of-living increases. However, it rarely happens two years in a row. The other purpose of the annual appraisal meeting is to discuss the goals and objectives for the upcoming year, and any performance modifications to achieve them. It's really important for a person to understand exactly what is expected of him, and what impact his performance may have on his base pay. As far as I'm concerned, the underpinning of respect for the individual is the performance appraisal process. An honest, straightforward discussion of a person's strengths and weaknesses forms the cornerstone of the IBM merit pay philosophy.

Breaking the Bank

Each year, IBM wants to present an incentive package that will treat everyone evenhandedly and will do its job – that is, motivate. In a nutshell, it works like this: every regional manager begins the fiscal year with a new quota and a set of goals to achieve. His quota is split up among his branch managers. Each branch manager then divides his quota among the marketing managers who report to him. The marketing managers make the final quota allocations, determining the bogey for each marketing rep. If this sounds a little like the Abbott and Costello 'Who's on first' routine, believe me, it's worse. We have tens of thousands of territories, and no two are alike.

There is a lot to factor into each quota: the size of the territory, the types of customers, their potential to expand, the kind of systems they can use, their service requirements, the rep's involvement in team projects, the conditions affecting the marketplace, product availability. There's more, but you get the idea. To complicate matters, no one is simply handed his quota. At each level, the factors and sometimes the numbers are debated. Think of this as a tops-down plan with bottoms-up input. The key philosophical point is that each individual, regardless of job level, is being measured against the same set of factors.

There are two basic quotas each person must deal with: one for products and one for installations, which is really revenue growth. They are the critical factors in determining how much money, over salary, these tens of thousands of people will receive by the time the curtain falls at the end of the year. The salesperson has mighty good reasons to sell as much as he can, and to install everything he sells.

The system may seem cumbersome, but it's complex only because IBM wants to be absolutely fair to the people in the field, and to the company too. It could be simplified but in this case simpler isn't better, because streamlining would eliminate the aspects that make one territory different from another.

Mistakes are made, by setting the goals either too high or too low. When that happens, there are adjustments, sometimes to the delight of the reps. But other times things happen unexpectedly, things that could blow the reps away. Management has to deal with reality; it can't simply say, 'Oops, sorry. We set the quotas, and you're stuck with them.' Whether a war breaks out, or the economy takes a nosedive, or there's an Arab oil embargo, the quotas have to be realistic. At the local level, the rep's earnings shouldn't be wiped out because his major account went bankrupt. Nor should he become rich simply because a major customer moved into his territory just as the fiscal year was coming to a close.

To cover unusual circumstances, each person's annual sales plan has built into it a safety net that can be implemented by each manager. Changes in the quotas, though necessary at times, are not made easily or frequently. IBM wants its people to believe in and respect the sales package they receive. It doesn't want them to think that the numbers delivered at the beginning of the year are just a starting point and that they'll fluctuate throughout the next twelve months. IBM plays hardball, but plays it equitably.

What about the service the company is so proud of? Where is the dollar incentive for all that hard work?

This will take some explaining. First, it's part of the salary, and the true payback comes from having a satisfied customer. But there is also a takeback provision. Specifically, when a customer cancels or discontinues any IBM equipment, all previously paid commissions are charged back to the marketing rep presently handling the account. While this sounds harsh, it serves as a key factor in making sure field people are paying attention to their customers, even during periods when little selling or installation is taking place. This approach centers on a corporate purpose of maintaining old customers, creating new ones, and making people want to do business with IBM through value-added selling.

IBM simply doesn't want to lose any business, and when it does, it investigates why. Monthly win-loss reports were prepared by the domestic and international marketing divisions from information supplied by their branch managers. These reports highlighted the significant wins as well as the circumstances that precipitated a major revenue or key customer loss. They were signed by division presidents and sent to IBM's top line management, with copies distributed to other high-ranking executives. It is distasteful, besides being embarrassing, to report a key loss, knowing that it will be reviewed, analyzed and evaluated by upper management. The idea is not to 'headhunt' but to understand the problems and take whatever action is necessary to prevent a pattern of losses from developing.

At the beginning of each year, everybody complains that the quotas are too high. It's the natural thing to do and I did it too when I was a rep. However, when the year's over and all the numbers are in, management looks pretty smart. During my entire career, I can remember only one year when we ever came in short of quota. I don't mean that every individual made his or hers, but the cumulative numbers were always there.

Historically, 65 to 75 percent of IBM's people go over the top each year. Five to 10 percent usually break the bank. Of those who don't make 100 percent of their quota, only a few are in trouble. Most make it the next year and do OK. Under 4 percent of IBM's marketing people are asked to leave involuntarily each year, and unsatisfactory sales performance is only one of the causes.

Throughout the year, extra commissions are offered over and above the quota program. These bonuses are initiated by headquarters management, usually in cooperation with the engineering/manufacturing divisions. They are used to help kick off a new product, enhance an existing program or gain momentum during a soft quarter. They certainly help energize the salespeople and, at the same time, put something extra into their wallets and pocketbooks.

When the subject of commissions has come up in a discussion with people outside IBM, I've often been asked: 'Doesn't your program put a lot of pressure on your reps? To expect a company rep to earn 50 percent of income in commissions is rather unusual.' It's true. However, the program applies pressure on *everybody*, not just the rep. But it's the kind of pressure that makes people work harder, and it is hoped, smarter. Making people reach is a positive thing. When an incentive program is working properly, it helps propel a person at a healthy pace throughout the year.

It's wonderful when you have motivations and

incentives on your side. It makes you stretch. Having run five miles a day for the past twelve years, I know the truth in the old French saying: 'One can go a long way after one is tired.' I'd add: 'But only when one is motivated.'

The Payoff

Just as a company cannot strive for excellence without putting pressure on itself, it cannot expect its people to be self-starters, innovators and company-minded unless it is generous in its appreciation of them. IBM demands a lot from its people, and understands the need to openly demonstrate its appreciation for those who work to achieve excellence. There's a broad range of appreciation, from a night on the town given to a rep by a marketing manager, to several thousands of dollars handed out by the head of a division.

Awards and rewards are distributed by every level of line management throughout the company. The higher the manager's position, the more money he has budgeted for this purpose.

Earlier, I mentioned the administrative person who received a wheelbarrowful of money for doing an exceptional job. When I was vice-president of the Data Processing Division, I praised one of the top marketing reps in front of an audience of several hundred of our people. Warren Hume, the division president, was very impressed with what I had to say about this person. He pulled me aside to find out a little more about him. Then Warren grabbed the microphone and announced, 'You've just heard a story about an outstanding performance by an outstanding person.' Turning to the rep, he continued, 'When you return to your office, waiting for you will be a check for five thousand dollars!' The whole thing was impromptu, and it brought down the house. A president's award isn't usually a spur-of-the-moment thing. It's usually decided upon after reviewing recommendations submitted by all the branch and regional offices in his jurisdiction. It might, for example, be in recognition of what IBM calls a significant win — that's when a new account is acquired, or a competitive winback is achieved, or a new application breakthrough occurs.

Serious about encouraging its people to feed it with suggestions, IBM is happy to give significant cash awards for those that are implemented. Awards have been given for ideas that improved the administrative process, enhanced products and reduced costs on the manufacturing floor. Ideas that pay off may be for such things as a new packaging technique that better protects a product, or a simplified process to more efficiently process an order.

A formalized corporate suggestion program exists, and a special department reviews each employee's submission, before sending it to the facility that will consider its practicability and dollar value. If the suggestion is adopted, the individual receives up to 25 percent of the accrued savings during the first two years of its use. The money involved can be tremendous — as high as six figures.

One of the first big-money ideas came from an employee in San Jose. He suggested the use of a wave soldering machine instead of hand soldering for logic card assembly. The company listened and cut a twenty-five-minute operation down to three seconds. He received a $100,000 bonus.

A service rep in Minneapolis saved the company over $1 million with his suggestion that a clip be added to the electronic 75 typewriter. His idea relieved wear on the rocker and earned him $100,000.

A contract specialist, also from Minneapolis, suggested an audit and control procedure that earned her $100,000.

An associate cost engineer from IBM Canada saved the company $70 million in two years with his suggested change in producing the serial number identifications that appear on every product. His idea was simple enough: stop stamping, start labelling. It made him a lot of money.

The IBM Suggestion Plan has been good for both the company and the employees who submitted useful ideas. The numbers are truly impressive: The company saved $300 million between 1975 and 1984, thanks to the suggestions of its employees, and it paid $60 million in awards to those who had the ideas. This doesn't just happen. IBM actively encourages its employees to get involved, to realize that their ideas count and will be respected. A twenty-two-page booklet, 'Your Ideas Have Value', that describes the company's Suggestion Plan is circulated throughout the company. In his introduction to its most recent edition, IBM CEO John Akers wrote: 'Today, one of our business goals is to be the most efficient in everything we do. Another goal is to achieve the highest quality for our products. To meet these goals, we will need imaginative and cost-saving ideas more than ever before. I encourage you, therefore, to look for better ways to run the business — and to submit your suggestions.'

It's no wonder that IBM has what may be the world's

most active suggestion box. Incidentally, every suggestion is acknowledged. If the idea is rejected, the participant receives an explanatory letter. No one is ever made to feel his or her idea is foolish or not taken seriously. The ideas *may be* important; the participant's feelings *are* important.

Another innovative program I recall was the Eagle Award, given to marketing reps who set new sales records in their division. The 'best of the best' were thus honored – less than one hundred people who attained new highs in performance. Besides the attention and publicity accompanying so significant an award, the winners received a check for $5,000 and a beautiful trophy.

Two of IBM's most prestigious recognition programs are the Corporate Technical Award and the new IBM Fellows. In 1984, IBM recognized the contributions of 259 technical professionals, including seventy-nine who shared a record $2.7 million in awards. The largest award – $1.78 million – went to two teams, comprising forty-eight employees, who worked to bring about the success of the IBM personal computer and the 3880 Direct Access Storage Device. Also, five new IBM Fellows were named, bringing to eighty-eight the number appointed since 1963. Chosen for their accomplishments in engineering, programming and science, IBM Fellows are free to pursue their own projects for a five-year period. The title is retained for life.

Awards You Can't Put in the Bank

Money isn't the only thing that motivates people. Almost anything that bolsters self-esteem can work. I don't mean that compliments or titles or certificates will satisfy a person who can't pay his bills – not for long, they won't – but they're a wonderful adjunct to a decent money package.

Each time an IBM rep achieves his annual quota, he becomes a member of the Hundred Percent Club. He doesn't have to brag about his results; his membership in the club is well publicized throughout the company. Among his peers he's recognized as a high achiever.

There's no doubt in my mind that a survey of new reps would show that their first goal, after being assigned a territory, is not to make 'a lot of money' but to achieve membership in the Hundred Percent Club. A rep who has failed to make it for three years probably won't get a chance to go for it in the fourth.

The top 10 percent of successful salespeople are elevated to the Golden Circle and their achievement is acknowledged throughout the entire organization, worldwide. They and their spouses are invited to a convention in a place such as Bermuda or Hawaii, and given full VIP treatment. Their celebrity status becomes known throughout the company and industry. At this meeting, it's not unusual to hear the spouse say, 'You better bring me back here next year.'

Honoring those who do superior work is not only motivation for them to continue their high-level performance but also a strong incentive for others. A company can't be *too* appreciative of its high achievers. Organizations that take them for granted don't deserve to keep them.

Is It All Worthwhile?

It takes a great deal of thought, lots of trial and error, and many man-hours to come up with the pay package for our marketing people. There are certainly easier ways to do it – straight salary or maybe a salary with a token incentive. But what IBM is doing must be OK.

For one thing, the company doesn't want to lose good people because of money. Its jobs should be the best-paying in the industry. More than that, actually: they should be the best-paying in any industry – for comparable work. Regular surveys indicate that IBM stays ahead of both its direct competitors and other industries. It's obvious even without the surveys, because so very few IBMers ever leave for other opportunities.

It's rare when the company doesn't exceed its objectives – which are never understated. IBM's growth has been one of the most dramatic ever, and everyone knows that well-motivated people are responsible.

I'm convinced that every facet of the compensation package works. At times, it seems difficult to implement because there is a package tailor-made for every individual. Even so, it's worth it. It works because the company is not trying to nickel-and-dime anyone, only to reward people for a job well done. Compensation and motivation serve to enhance marketing as a professional career.

10

The Entrepreneurial Spirit

Good people need room to develop. They have to find their own voice . . . each IBMer is a businessperson working within the framework of the company structure.

The same entrepreneurial spirit that makes new proprietary business ventures happen is necessary in the corporate establishment, as well. It isn't needed only when a business is being formulated. No matter how big or how old the corporation is, if it's going to respond to change and continually grow, it must keep alive the original spirit that transformed someone's idea and dream into the reality of a business.

Sadly, for too many companies, the daring and the enthusiasm generated during their beginnings seem impossible to sustain. Overburdened and stifled by the bureaucracy they created, many mature organizations move with the agility of an obese, arthritic giant. They're not as excited by adventure as they used to be. What turns them on is the idea of a safe, comfortable place to rest. Unfortunately for them, they have to be alert and alive just to survive, which is no easy feat in today's competitive world. These companies are usually led by decisionmakers who have lost some of their intuitiveness, and don't trust what's left of it. They don't want to make a move unless they are absolutely, positively certain that they've covered their backsides. They demand more and more facts on which to base their decisions, finally settling only for what they are convinced is a sure thing. But the less adventurous they become, the more difficult it is for them to discern even the safest path. It all boils down to too much emphasis on minimizing the risk rather than maximizing the opportunity. In time, the planning and decisionmaking processes take on a life of their own, engendering open-ended exercises that eventually self-destruct. I have no idea how much corporate time and money are wasted on plans that never had a chance of getting off the drawing board, but it's a crime against employees and stockholders who depend on dynamic leadership. Those leaders who have lost the entrepreneurial spirit should step aside, making room for those who desperately want to express theirs. Of course, people in power rarely step aside voluntarily. That's why IBM's policy of having officers relinquish certain jobs at age sixty is so effective. It gives the people at the top a marvelous opportunity to do some deep self-analysis; to examine their motives for wanting to stay in a position that may require the derring-do of a young, hungry, highly motivated entrepreneur.

Risk-takers are important not only at the top of the organization, but throughout all levels of the company. It's difficult to develop a nurturing environment for corporate entrepreneurialism if the spirit is missing at the top. Happily for those of us who came to IBM with the need to do more than simply make a living, we found a place that welcomed people with ideas, who were willing to argue with the managers, administrators and executives to get their ideas into motion.

People like these cause problems, create turmoil and confound the conservatives who want peace and serenity in their organization. But they build companies; and it took a lot of them to build an IBM.

Greatness Is Enduring

From the beginning, Tom Watson, Sr, knew that you couldn't develop corporate entrepreneurs if you encumbered your employees with an enervating bureaucratic structure. Watson was no theorist, but he knew intuitively that an overgrown bureaucracy strangles creativity and the spirit needed to take chances. His solution was to construct his company in such a way that no employee would have to deal with a giant structure, no matter how big it might grow. He succeeded. When I joined the company, it was a $250 million business and it didn't 'feel' big. If I had been employed by a company a fraction of the size of IBM, I would probably have had to deal with a much bigger bureaucracy. Even today, a new employee coming into IBM – now a $50 billion corporation – finds himself in a small-business atmosphere. In part, this is true because the company never allows its branches to get too big; and, regardless of any function, a manager supervises about ten to twelve people, rarely more. This way, no one gets lost. A budding entrepreneur is quickly recognized and encouraged. The manager not only is expected to nurture this type of person but is evaluated on the success of the nurturing. The result is a working environment charged with excitement, creative energy, and commitment.

Any company that is experiencing the doldrums, or

suffers from negativism, tension, frustration and unrest, should take a hard, long look at companies like IBM. That doesn't mean there are no disappointments or frustrations in IBM, but its overriding attitude is one of dynamic optimism: If you're the best, anything is possible. And you can be the best if you're willing to make a total commitment to that end.

The Corporate Rep

When I was president of the Data Processing Division, we came up each year with a different theme for the sales force. In 1969, the theme was *entrepreneurship*. Some people strongly objected: 'We should avoid this subject. It might encourage some of our best people to leave IBM and start their own businesses.' Others felt that it made no sense to talk about entrepreneurship in a publicly owned corporation, because the dictionary definition excluded anyone who was not risking his own money and did not have a proprietary interest in the business. I disagreed with the worriers at IBM, and with colleagues who couldn't see beyond Webster's definition.

Of course, the IBM rep does not take the same financial risks an independent agent takes – that is, he's assured a substantial part of his potential income, his expenses are covered and he's the recipient of a number of company benefits. On the other hand, the corporate rep has responsibilities and obligations, and is held accountable in a way that the independent is not. Being self-employed, the independent agent may lose a customer, or twenty, and can't be fired. Both invest their time in a career, and both take their share of risks.

That IBM reps receive at least half of their income in commissions – a high number for a corporate salesperson – attracts the kind of rep the company wants: an ambitious person with an entrepreneurial spirit. But the person is also expected to give the kind of service IBM's customers have a right to expect. The entire training program, starting with the first day, encourages reps to be creative, innovative and industrious.

Everything possible is done to eliminate bureaucratic obstacles that might stand in their way. The time clock everyone was required to punch was eliminated in the 1950s. Until the 1960s, every rep was required to submit a weekly work plan. There was a real celebration when that ended. I never thought it made sense for our reps to report into the office every morning, before their first call; no matter how it was rationalized, it was simply a way for a sales manager to make sure that his people were awake and ready for work. I'd tell my people: 'You were hired because we believed you could do the job. Nobody's going to coddle you. But if you're not producing, I'm going to take a hard look to see what's wrong. I'll monitor your performance, and when you do well, you'll be applauded and rewarded. The truth is, you'll probably see less of me when you're doing a good job. It's when you're not performing well that I'll be around, trying to find out why.'

Good people need room to develop. They have to find their own voice. Their growth will be stunted if they're too tightly supervised. They have to find their own style – a comfortable natural delivery. But an operating system that's rooted in suspicion and insecurity is certain to squeeze the spontaneity out of their performance. My advice to good people who find themselves fighting a losing battle for the right to personal expression is *run for your life!* Enthusiastic, bright, creative people turn sour under dull, self-conscious management that's protected by a bureaucratic system with no sensibility at all.

To promote the entrepreneurial spirit, especially throughout the sales and marketing divisions, IBM's management must take its share of risks. The company must give its salespeople a sense of territorial proprietorship. They need to be granted as much authority and responsibility as they can handle, as quickly as possible. That means getting out of the way of their decisionmaking, once the power is delegated. The corporate entrepreneur, like the independent, needs the freedom to experiment. He will make his share of mistakes and learn how to deal with them. If he is successful, the benefit to the company is immeasurable. He adds to the creative flow that energizes the entrepreneurial corporation.

In a sense, each IBMer is a business person working within the framework of the company structure. As reps gain experience, they are more and more on their own. At the same time, they enjoy the benefit of having the company's wide spectrum of support and services. One of the real tests is how creatively they can utilize everything available to them. In this respect, the corporate entrepreneur has a decided edge over the independent. The success of our rep hinges on teamwork and his ability to marshal the talent and expertise of a variety of specialists. His job is very much like that of a general manager with an abundance of resources. He must be wisely selective in the use of these resources and coordinate them with the needs of the customer. How well he meshes the available expertise to the problems he's dealing with will be a measure of his own ingenuity.

In order for the 'spirit' to permeate the entire organization, everyone must share the same set of objectives. All must work together, that's true, but at the same time they must have a very strong sense of their individual involvement and contribution. A professional baseball team might be a good analogy: Nine entrepreneurs take the field, each covering his own territory, each with his own special expertise – independent performers, each dependent on the rest for the best results. There might be better analogies: a Dixieland band, maybe; a half-dozen free spirits . . . You get the point.

In IBM's marketing format, each rep has his own business base, made up of a block of accounts that he inherited when he took over the territory, and perhaps a list of prospective accounts that he will try to sell. It's his patch. What he earns depends on how profitably he manages the business. The rep has a business to manage for IBM, but so do the marketing managers, the branch managers, the regional managers. As a rule, the closer they are to the customer, the further they are from bureaucracy.

It's pleasant when people who work together in an office do so in harmony. If they don't get along, if they pull in different directions or have problems communicating, the quality of their work life will suffer. In addition, how well they understand one another and how well they work together can have a direct bearing on their paychecks. To get their job done properly, and have the commissions rolling in, they must all march to the same drummer. This calls for a bottoms-up input and a tops-down plan, with everyone working toward the same goal.

Career Paths for Corporate Reps

The motto of most ambitious employees, whatever their position, is 'I'll move up or move on'. That's compatible with the attitude of many success-driven companies, which say to their people, 'You'll move up or you're out.' The assumption is that people who work hard and strive for excellence will in time outgrow their position and be elevated. If they're not, they will become bored and feel wasted.

Promotions usually mean an immediate salary increase and greater earning potential. That's very important to most ambitious people. But salespeople are in a special situation. They don't have to move up to make more. At least, those who work for IBM don't. Plenty of IBM reps earn more money than line managers do, and I think that's the way it should be. I'm delighted when 10 to 15 percent of the sales force earn more than their bosses.

A professional sales force is vital to the success of a marketing organization. IBM is truly aware of that, and as you have read in these pages, it does everything possible to translate that awareness into concrete satisfaction for the reps. They are treated as heroes by everyone in the company – all the way up to the chairman of the board.

Although most of IBM's top-level management

people started off in sales, selling skills aren't a surefire indicator that a person will make a terrific manager. While it's imperative to conduct an ongoing talent search for potential managers, it's also important to keep the vast majority of salespeople in their territories, and happy. Customers don't usually like it when they lose their rep. Not every salesperson wants to be a branch manager or a division president, but everyone wants as much recognition and job satisfaction as possible. So to build into the salesperson's career a theme of progression, the marketing rep, who started off as a trainee, can become an account rep, an advisory rep, a senior marketing rep, a consultant. Each of these titles is recognition of the salesperson's growth, professionalism and value to the company. But they are more than just titles; each of them carries a more lucrative reward system. IBM believes that a successful sales career is in itself a significant achievement – an entrepreneurial achievement – that mustn't be taken for granted.

The Corporate Beauty Contest

The successful entrepreneur is by nature a talented, creative person. He or she has qualities that can enhance any company, if they are recognized, nurtured and exercised. Too many of the people running businesses today don't understand the importance of ferreting out the talent in their work force. Many times, management misunderstands this type of person. They are often difficult to read, and management therefore builds fences around them to squelch the creativity each company needs so badly. *Undercover the talent in your organization before you drive it away*. When people in your company spend their off-hours acting in community theater, or taking art classes, but do only what's expected of them on the job, don't you wonder if you're providing them with the opportunity they need to express their talents from nine to five?

Creativity and other characteristics of the latent entrepreneur will emerge anytime they're given the opportunity to do so. So when IBM finds talented people it moves them around, to broaden their point of view. Management tries to discover just which position in the organization will allow that talent to flourish. A person who has had an engineering assignment might be transferred to a product planning position; or someone is moved from finance to personnel. The idea is to bring talent and need together, to cross-pollinate whenever possible, to make sure that creative people are dealt with creatively in the company.

Although many corporate entrepreneurs work best alone, their work with others affords insights into their managerial and organizational abilities. When these people come to IBM management's attention, they are frequently assigned to task forces where they can be informally observed and evaluated. As corporate vice-president of marketing, I often invited five to ten field reps to spend two or three days on a task force assignment. We evaluated their reactions to confidential marketing information, and asked for input on such things as sales plan policies, marketing practices and product development. From this group I could easily find people ready for management positions.

Marketing people who have high management potential are often given key staff assignments lasting from one to three years. They are rotated between line and staff positions. This gives them the broadest possible exposure, to test their creativity and management skills in a variety of environments and situations. In these people identified and groomed for executive positions, the entrepreneurial spirit must burn brightly, if they are to run the corporation someday.

And as far as I'm concerned, field people are entrepreneurs. Whether they are branch managers, regional managers or division presidents, they are compensated, by and large, according to their bottom line, like the independent business owner. They have no guarantees. Each has his career on the line, all the time. Their performance is evaluated thoroughly; each paycheck is based on productivity. Continual poor results will bring down the corporate entrepreneur as quickly as it will bring down the business owner – probably more quickly.

Turning 'em Loose

IBM's interest in corporate entrepreneuring is more than simply developing an adventurous attitude or spirit, though the importance of that is certainly recognized. And it certainly isn't an exercise in semantics – trying to embrace 'entrepreneuring' because it's one of the hottest business buzzwords of the decade. IBMers never lose sight of the fact that their company is the product of one man's daring. IBM grew to its present size because of Tom Watson's ability to impart his entrepreneurial spirit to the tens of thousands of people who joined him. In the 1980s, some innovative programs were initiated to explore and test different types of corporate entrepreneuring. What's developed has been quite exciting. A number of independent, self-contained 'businesses' have been established within the company. These units don't function as divisions of IBM, and they don't need to interact with any other part of the company or rely on any of its resources — except for money and talent. What makes them so different from any other part of IBM is that they are not subject to the company's strategic planning and review processes. No five-year plans for them. No rigid rules or inflexible policies. A freewheeling management style is encouraged, and their autonomous boards are free to make decisions beyond what is typically permitted by the company. In short, all organizational roadblocks have been eliminated. The units are, of course, expected to abide by IBM's ethics and dedication to quality.

The people who operate these Independent Business Units come from all over IBM and are headed by key executives and officers. They are asked to develop new products and establish them in the proper marketplace. What's wanted is that they go into areas in need of special care and nurturing to grow. The hope is that after a period of maturing, the new business will be integrated into the corporate mainstream.

In 1985, there were fourteen Independent Business Units within IBM. One is Manufacturing Systems Products in Boca Raton, Florida, a unit in the field of robotics. Another is IBM Instruments Inc., in Danbury, Connecticut, a manufacturer of measuring devices. IBM Information Services, in Milford, Connecticut, is leading the company's extensive effort to develop its own computer software and is aggressively acquiring new programs from outsiders. If the Milford operation were a separate company, it would rank in the *Fortune* 500.

Perhaps the best example of an IBM 'business within a business' – the supersuccess story – is a little unit that was activated in 1980. Ten engineers were brought together under the leadership of Philip Estridge to start a new business. Four years later, this entrepreneurial unit of less than a dozen people had grown to $5 billion division of IBM, Entry Systems, employing ten thousand people in Boca Raton, Florida, and Austin, Texas. That's how the IBM PC began.

At the first meeting, the eleven were told, 'We want an IBM personal computer. We're already late, so you'll have to hurry. Do whatever you feel is necessary to get it done.' They were given the freedom to buy components from the outside, if they thought that was the way to go – to negotiate whatever terms and conditions made sense to them. Even pricing and distribution were left to their discretion. It worked. The IBM personal computer is here to stay, a major contributor to the industry.

The eleven people who began Entry Systems were experienced IBMers with proven track records. They were high achievers. But more than that, they were true entrepreneurs, who didn't hesitate to put their careers on the line when a challenging opportunity was presented. The real story, though, is that a huge corporation with a managerial organization that's bigger than some governments is able to *develop and nurture such entrepreneurs*. It has nothing to do with sales, profit, size or the kind of business one is in. It has everything to do with spirit, caring and trying your best to understand the people you work with.

The Royal Dissenters

The management of a company has to have its share of internal critics or else it has a tendency to get self-indulgent, fat and sloppy. Like most of us, I like to have things go my way, but I can't stand to work in a world of yes-men. They create an atmosphere that can lull you to sleep. I like people who care enough about what's going on to speak up when they don't like what they see. Of course, there are critics and there are *critics*, but even the worst of them are more stimulating than the best of the yes-men. The critic who has the most negative effect on me is the constant complainer – the cynic who gripes about everything but never offers a suggestion to help ward off the gloom and doom he forever forecasts. This guy isn't just a pain in the backside; he deadens one's responses to him. People turn him off; they don't listen to him. And a concern of his that may deserve some serious attention gets shrugged off. Another type of critic is the loyal dissenter. He's pretty good at spotting trouble, or seeing a weakness in a program or plan, but he hates to rock the boat; so he keeps any solutions he may have to himself. Finally, there's the kind of complainer every organization needs: the *royal* dissenter. He or she offers not only a well-thought-out criticism but also a considered approach to dealing with the problem.

I have always encouraged my people to question, to probe, to express their concerns – to criticize. 'And when you do,' I've told them, 'try to be logical and calm; maintain your poise. Never be afraid of taking a stand. At the same time, be constructive; not abrasive and cynical. Don't turn every minor issue into a major one. When you decide to take me on, make sure that you have your facts straight, and be prepared to stand up for what you believe. Most of all, think in terms of *solution*.'

The more responsibility you carry, the more important it is for you to get your people to think in terms of what they would do if they were in your shoes. You want them to develop a proprietary attitude about the company. The last thing you want to do is inhibit them from expressing their criticisms. Don't chase them to the nearest bar, where they can commiserate, over drinks, about how bad things are.

Every company needs it royal dissenters. Like the corporate entrepreneurs, they are risk-takers. They're willing to stick their necks out and challenge the status quo. They'll do it again and again when they are convinced that they're right. They write letters to top management, and fill the suggestion boxes. These people believe that they have the right ideas, and they want to convey them. They don't care whom they're talking to. It could be one of their peers, or the chairman of the board. They're not afraid to stand up in a meeting and challenge a speaker; but when they do, they do it in a constructive way. They are those 'wild ducks' of business that Tom Watson, Jr, talks about. Their tenacious persistence – and guts – help keep a company young and exciting. In *In Search of Excellence*, they are singled out as the most important key to sustained innovative success in the excellent companies. Happily, IBM has always had its share of people who refused to fly in formation.

Knowing How Far to Let Out the Reins

I've heard people say, 'A good manager allows his people to fail.' This school of thought says that once you give responsibility to a subordinate, it becomes his project, and you must stay out of his way – even when you know that he's on the wrong track! I don't buy it. It's not my style to think: 'I know this guy is blowing it, but I have to allow him the luxury of fouling up.' You have to use common sense! Depending upon the size of the project, its failure could turn out to be too expensive for the organization. You needn't yank the rug from under the employee. Instead of taking away responsibility, assume the role of mentor. Guide him into making the necessary corrections that will get him back on track, and then get out of his way. Remember that you turned over the project to him in the first place because you identified him as a person with the entrepreneurial spirit. You don't want to kill that.

In part, your success with these people will be determined by your ability to know how far to let out the reins and when to pull them in; in knowing how to nurture creativity and at the same time avoid a predictable head-on collision with failure. Taking risks, as far as I'm concerned, is taking *calculated risks*, not foolish ones. Although many checks can be built into the system to cushion the downside of a new venture (I talked about them earlier), nothing is more important than the care that goes into the selection of a risk-taker, the person with the idea or the dream who is willing to put his career on the line.

By the time anyone at IBM makes it to the executive

suite, he's had more than his share of exposure to pressure situations. He's in a position to take risks, and is decisive and capable of acting on his convictions. Businesses that fail to develop entrepreneurs don't allow their lower and middle management to make tough decisions. They feel safer with consensus decisions; more comfortable with bureaucratic committees. In that type of company, an individual who climbs to a top managerial position has little or no risk-taking experience. He will not be an innovative or a daring leader.

During my thirty-four-year career with IBM, many tough touch-and-go decisions were made. At least five involved risks of tremendous magnitude. If the decisions were wrong, there would have been disastrous consequences for the company. Not one of the decisions was made because the company was 'in trouble,' nor were they reactions to sudden or unexpected forces. They were put into motion and implemented in the best of times for IBM, because the entrepreneurial spirit burns brightly anytime – if you have the kind of people who press for innovation and change, even when they'd never be faulted for relaxing and enjoying the present comfort. The five decisions I'm referring to have been mentioned earlier, but I'll run them by you in the context of this discussion: (1) IBM's switch from the punch-card system to stored programming; (2) the development and introduction of System/ 360, IBM's $5 billion gamble; (3) 'unbundling' – breaking down the prices of our products into their various components; (4) when IBM consolidated our three marketing divisions from a product-set approach into two customer-set organizations; (5) adopting alternative distribution systems into the marketing program.

While all these moves proved to be successful, at the time of its conception and implementation each involved risk taking of the highest order. Because they were initiated when it would have been easier for IBM to play its cards close to the vest, sitting tight, doing nothing, they were truly important acts of corporate entrepreneurialism. They won't be the last of IBM's bold, creative moves. You can bet on it.

Some Final Thoughts

In the Introduction, I suggested that any company of any size could emulate IBM's way. That's because the *way* IBM operates isn't expensive, nor is it exclusive. It deals, more than anything else, with people, their behavior and their values.

The company has grown to its great size, with incredible speed, because of its insatiable appetite to be the very best. That's the secret weapon. Of course, IBM makes useful products, but it's the quest for excellence that attracts and nurtures high achievers: young people whose ambitions are compatible with IBM's. The continual influx of this bright new talent keeps the company youthful, vibrant and light on its feet. But age is not a primary factor, since almost all of IBM's employees spend their entire professional career with the company, and stay on until retirement. Besides, whatever their age, IBM people are youthful, spirited and adventuresome.

I hope that *Fortune* magazine's annual survey for the past three years accurately reflects the business community's attitude about IBM. If IBM *is* America's most respected company, it's a good sign. Just as our children need honorable heroes for role models, so do the rest of us, including those who run corporate America. As far as I'm concerned, IBM does embody those traits and characteristics that are usually attributed to the American hero: honesty, intelligence, courage, strength, thoughtfulness and gentleness. The 'I' in IBM could stand for Integrity.

Although the company operates in the high-tech world of lightning-fast communication, it tries to project a voice that is soft, calm and friendly – not frantic or threatening or jargon-laden.

I wish all companies would talk to their people about such things as behavior and ethics, as IBM does. It didn't embarrass IBM to circulate this statement to its 400,000 employees:

> You are responsible for your actions, and this responsibility will not always be an easy one. The next time you have an ethical dilemma, you might try this test. Ask yourself: If the full glare of examination by associates, friends, even family, were to focus on your decision, would you remain comfortable with it? If you think you would, it probably is the right decision.

The three basic beliefs that guide every IBM action can be shared with anyone who's smart enough to grab on to them: *You must respect the dignity and rights of the individual. You must give the best possible service to the customer. You must pursue all tasks with the objective of accomplishing them in a superior way.* There it is, direct and uncomplicated. No one needs an MBA or a PhD to understand those three statements; nor does it take a *Fortune* 500 company to implement them.

All of us, including IBM, will be better off when this becomes the standard operating procedure for all US businesses. The sooner the better.

APPENDIX:

Excerpts from IBM's 'Business Conduct Guidelines'

(a booklet given every IBM employee)

Our company has an enviable reputation. People generally think of us as competent, successful and ethical. These three qualities are related. Our adherence to strict ethical standards has contributed, in a very direct way, to both the professionalism of our company and our success in the marketplace. Over the years, we have emphasized again and again that every employee is expected to act in accordance with the highest standards of ethics. This is still true today. And it will be true tomorrow.

* * *

Business today is being called upon as never before to explain its actions, provide reasons for its decisions and speak out clearly on where it stands on ethical behavior . . . it [is] essential in this time of questioning and testing that everyone – employees and their families, customers and competitors, friends as well as critics – know just where IBM stands on basic ethical issues . . . If there is a single, overriding message in these guidelines, it is that IBM expects every employee to act, in every instance, according to the highest standards of business conduct. Ultimately, in every business decision – as in personal ones – the responsibility is yours.

* * *

We depend on you to do the right thing; right for both you and the company. It is no exaggeration to say that IBM's reputation is in your hands.

* * *

First, there is the law. It must be obeyed. But the law is the minimum. You must act ethically.

* * *

Fair competition. The dictionary puts it very simply: Compete – to contend with another for acknowledgment, for a prize, for a profit.
Ethical. Dealing with morals or the principles of morality; pertaining to right and wrong in conduct. These simple definitions describe what IBM requires of those who represent it in the marketplace. It asks them to compete – vigorously, energetically, untiringly. But it also insists they compete ethically, honestly and fairly, in accordance with basic principles of morality. Clearly, there are situations that individual IBM employees confront only in business, and for those IBM provides detailed guidelines. But IBM employees who deal directly with customers must be guided first by the knowledge that ethics and morality are the same at work as at home. There is no special, less restrictive set of ethics for business, no easier 'marketplace morality'.

* * *

From the very beginning, IBM has relied on one thing above all to sell its products: excellence. It always has been IBM's policy to provide the best possible products and services to customers, and to sell on the merits of our own products and services – not by disparaging competitors, or their products and services. In short, sell IBM. Disparaging remarks include not only false statements, but also information which is misleading or simply unfair. Even factually correct material can be disparaging if it's derogatory and irrelevant to the particular sales situation. This includes casting doubt on a competitor's capabilities or making unfair comparisons. Subtle hints or innuendos are wrong, too. For instance, asking customer or prospect what they've heard about the competitor's maintenance service. If your objective is to focus the prospect's attention on a known problem, don't do it.

*　*　*

As a matter of practice, if a competitor already has a firm order from a customer for an application, we don't market IBM products or service for that application before the competitor has installed others. However, this is a complicated subject. For example, it is often difficult to determine whether a firm order actually exists. Letters of intent, free trials, conditional agreements and the like usually are not firm orders. Unconditional contracts are. Generally speaking, if a firm order does not exist, an IBM marketing representative may sell. When a situation is unclear or if there is any doubt, seek advice from your business practices or legal function.

*　*　*

You should also be sensitive to how you use information about other companies, which often includes information about individuals. Those other companies and individuals are rightly concerned about their reputations and privacy. Adverse information of no business use should not even be retained in your files. And what information you do retain should be treated with discretion.

* * *

Don't boast. IBM should not try to get business by trading on its size or success or its position in the industry. That means no boasting to customers about how much money we spend on research or product development, or how many systems engineers we have available throughout the company to work with customers. It is all right to talk about the quality of IBM's products or services. Resources and people represent a commitment to the customer that, for example, an area education facility is staffed and equipped to provide the customer's education requirements. That's not boasting bigness; it's relevant to that particular customer's needs.

* * *

Don't make misrepresentations to anyone you deal with. If you believe the other person may have misunderstood you, correct any misunderstanding you find exists. Honesty is integral to ethical behavior, and trustworthiness is essential for good, lasting relationships.

* * *

Everyone you do business with is entitled to fair and evenhanded treatment. This is true whether you are buying, selling or performing in any other capacity for IBM . . . You must treat all suppliers fairly. In deciding among competing suppliers, weight all the facts impartially, whether you are in purchasing, a branch office or some other part of the business, and whether you are buying millions of parts or a single, small repair job. Whether or not you directly influence decisions involving business transactions, you must avoid doing anything that might create the appearance that a customer or a supplier has 'a friend at IBM' who exerts special influence on its behalf.

* * *

Seeking reciprocity is contrary to IBM policy and in some cases may even be unlawful. You may not do business with a supplier of goods or of services (a bank, for example) on condition that it agrees to use IBM products or services. Do not tell a prospective customer that IBM deserves the business because of our own purchases from his or her organization. This does not mean we cannot be supplied by an IBM customer. It does mean that IBM's decision to use a supplier must be independent of that supplier's decision to use IBM products or services.

* * *

It is IBM practice not to disclose, discuss or sell IBM products before their announcement. For IBM to reveal anything about unannounced products – whether equipment, programs, or services – to a prospect or customer could be viewed by a competitor as unfair. In addition, pre-announcement disclosure could reach other customers and impact sales of IBM's existing product line, or jeopardize IBM copyright or patent positions. Besides, it is always possible for technical difficulties during product development to result in cancellation or postponement of the new product.

Nondisclosure also means that an IBM representative may not attempt to delay a customer decision to order competitive equipment by hinting that a new IBM product is under development. (There are exceptions to the nondisclosure rule, as in the case of national interest, or when a user works with IBM to develop new products, programs, or services. For such cases, there are careful procedures which must be closely followed.)

Index

INDEX

The Colours of Your Mind

The Revolutionary Approach to Managing Your Thinking Style

Jerry Rhodes and Sue Thame

Skilful thinking is vital to success. Yet too often the way we think is muddled, inappropriate and ineffective. In this brilliantly original, clear and pragmatic account, top-class business consultants, Jerry Rhodes and Sue Thame, show that this is because thinking is intangible, invisible.

The Colours of Your Mind offers a simple, thoroughly researched code or language for recognising our mental faculties in action. Through questionnaires, exercises, examples and illustrations, the authors show that using colours to label our thought processes – red for facts and realities, blue for judgement and opinions, green for ingenuity and imagination – can help us penetrate the very workings of our minds, our behaviour, emotions and intellect.

Find out your own personal style of dealing with the world, and why people deal with you as they do. This new, universal language of colours will help you maximize your strengths, improve work satisfaction and build successful relations with colleagues, friends and family. Now a widely used management training tool, colour coding is sure to revolutionise the way you think, work and live.

'What insights into our behaviour!' Rennie Fritchie, Chair, Gloucester Health Authority (NHS)

FONTANA PAPERBACKS

Keep Going For It!

Living the Life of an Entrepreneur

Victor Kiam is going for it again! Just in case you thought it might be time to take it easy, the king of entrepreneurs has put together a second colourful cocktail of advice and anecdote to keep you up and running with the best of them.

Victor Kiam is know to millions as 'the man who bought the company' – the man who liked the Remington shaver so much that he bought the entire corporation that made it. He took a loss-maker and made it profitable – then wrote *Going For It!*, the bestseller that explained how it was done. End of story? By no means, Victor Kiam is an entrepreneur, a man who knows that if you stop developing you're not just standing still – you're going backwards.

In *Keep Going For It!* Victor Kiam explains how to succeed as an entrepreneur – and then keep on succeeding. Whether your pitch is a market stall or a conglomerate's boardroom the principle is the same – recognize your potential, maximize that potential and keep on maximizing that potential. Just what should be done when it seems every tangible asset's been exhausted and a project still won't rise off the ground? What happens when it seems that every potential buyer for your brilliant new idea just can't see past the first trifling hurdle? What can be done when a new scheme falls flat – even crashes into failure? Who should win when your home life and your business life are set on a collision course? *Keep Going For It!* offers hardnosed solutions to each of the above – and more – with specific examples drawn from a lifetime of successful risk-taking.

If you're a true entrepreneur then business is *the* great adventure – but only if you *Keep Going For It!*

FONTANA PAPERBACKS